Astrologically
Incorrect for Lovers

Other books by Terry Marlowe and published by Adams Media:

Astrologically Incorrect

Astrologically Incorrect for Lovers

*Slightly wicked advice for
seducing any sign of the zodiac*

Terry Marlowe

Adams Media
Avon, Massachusetts

Published by Adams Media, an F+W Publications Company
57 Littlefield Street
Avon, MA 02322
www.adamsmedia.com

ISBN 10: 1-59337-364-3
ISBN 13: 978-1-59337-364-1

Printed in Canada.

J I H G F E D C B

Library of Congress Cataloging-in-Publication Data
Marlowe, Terry.
Astrologically incorrect for lovers / Terry Marlowe.
p.   cm.
ISBN-13: 978-1-59337-364-1
ISBN-10: 1-59337-364-3
1. Astrology and sex. 2. Love—Miscellanea. I. Title.
BF1729.S4M36 2006
133.5'864677—dc22
2006028191

This publication is designed to provide accurate and authoritative information with regard to the subject matter covered. It is sold with the understanding that the publisher is not engaged in rendering legal, accounting, or other professional advice. If legal advice or other expert assistance is required, the services of a competent professional person should be sought.

—From a *Declaration of Principles* jointly adopted by a Committee of the
American Bar Association and a Committee of Publishers and Associations

Many of the designations used by manufacturers and sellers to distinguish their product are claimed as trademarks. Where those designations appear in this book and Adams Media was aware of a trademark claim, the designations have been printed with initial capital letters.

This book is available at quantity discounts for bulk purchases.
For information, please call 1-800-289-0963.

contents

introduction vii

HOW TO USE YOUR LOVER'S—OR FUTURE LOVER'S—
SUN SIGN TO GET THE MOST OUT OF THIS BOOK

sun sign dates 1

1. the enamored egoist 2

ARIES—THE RAM, MARCH 20–APRIL 20

2. the bullheaded hedonist 22

TAURUS—THE BULL, APRIL 21–MAY 21

3. the dynamic duo 44

GEMINI—THE TWINS, MAY 22–JUNE 21

4. the cosseting crustacean 60

CANCER—THE CRAB, JUNE 22–JULY 23

5. *the enthroned beloved* 78
   LEO—THE LION, JULY 24–AUGUST 23

6. *the velcro virgin* 98
   VIRGO—THE VIRGIN, AUGUST 24–SEPTEMBER 23

7. *the randy romantic* 114
   LIBRA—THE SCALES, SEPTEMBER 24–OCTOBER 23

8. *the sadistic seducer* 132
   SCORPIO—THE SCORPION OR THE EAGLE, OCTOBER 24–NOVEMBER 22

9. *the absentee admirer* 148
   SAGITTARIUS—THE ARCHER, NOVEMBER 23–DECEMBER 21

10. *the potentate of protocol* 162
    CAPRICORN—THE GOAT, DECEMBER 22–JANUARY 20

11. *the humanitarian heartthrob* 176
    AQUARIUS—THE WATER BEARER, JANUARY 21–FEBRUARY 19

12. *the shape-shifting soul mate* 190
    PISCES—THE FISHES, FEBRUARY 20–MARCH 19

conclusion 205

introduction

how to use your lover's— or future lover's— sun sign to get the most out of this book

Romeo died for it. Guinevere got her last glimpse of Camelot while she was being tied to the stake for it. What was the catalyst for their common sacrifice? Love.

Maybe they had bad luck. Or just bad advice.

Romeo could have told the Montague and Capulet clans to butt out. Guinevere might have had a civilized chat with Arthur and told him she wanted to run off with Lancelot. And if he gave her a hard time, she could've retained a good royal divorce lawyer with the bravery to tell Arthur exactly where he could stick Excalibur.

By using astrology to obtain sound, useful advice spiced with attitude, modern folks can get not only what they want from their lovers, but also what they need—without the lover ever suspecting it. Some people call this method manipulative or unfair. Smart folks call it "astute people management."

To skillfully weave your way through the mating maze, first read the chapter about the lover you wish to manipulate. For example, if you're a wily Virgo who just met a delicious Leo, read the Leo chapter to find out what you can expect, how to attract the Lion, how to handle a committed relationship, and what you should and should not do.

Later, if you tire of him or her, you can try one of fifteen ways to leave your loser. (This Leo *must* be a loser. Otherwise you'd still want to be in the relationship.)

At the end of each chapter, there's a quick reference guide to show you how well you match up with each of the other signs.

It's a good idea to read the chapter about your own sun sign. For example, Virgos can pick up clues about how someone might be manipulating *them*. Remember, though, that this chapter was written *about* you, not *for* you, and chances are you'll think it's off the mark. Maybe you'll even find it unkind. Swallow your pride, open your brilliant mind, and you'll learn that there's truth to the trite axiom, "The best offense is a good defense."

A Tour Around the Zodiac

How would you know which person you want if you're unfamiliar with her sign's characteristics? If you want a spontaneous lover who'll whirl you off to an unknown destination, she probably won't be found with her nose buried in a book and her hand clasped around her daybook to ensure she stays on schedule. This is where astrology can help. Decide on the personality type of the one you want, then search for a star sign to match.

To glean information from a sun sign you must first know what it is. Of course, not all those born under the same astrological sign have the same personalities. Complete horoscopes can reveal all the idiosyncrasies, peculiarities, and pesky, deep-seated neuroses that keep therapists' couches occupied year round. This book provides additional general information about each different astrological sign to help you attract whom you want, when you want. Then, you can get them to do what you want—whether they like it or not.

The sun sign may provide only part of the complete picture, but there's still a great deal of value in it. You may not have the whole story, but at least you'll know from the astrological version of *Cliffs Notes* what book you're reading.

Looking for Love
(Also Known as Shopping for a Date or Mate)

We're about to go shopping for potential lovers.

"No prob," you declare. "I'm a pro. From grocery co-ops to auto parts stores, I've shopped 'em all."

Yes, you've braved the bulk-food bins to search for pine nuts and pepitas, and carefully chosen which frozen foods will grace your freezer's shelves. At the auto parts store, you scoped out the location of antifreeze and whisked windshield wiper blades into your basket.

However, go pack your imagination, because we're going on a trip to a different destination—the Mate Store. (Historically, this has also been referred to as "cruising the club scene.") In this store, the guests are gender neutral. *Remember: in love, as in politics, what you see isn't necessarily what you get.*

Imagine a place where people can say anything on their minds without getting bopped by the bad-manners bouncer for being a jerk. "What freedom," you observe as you open the door and peer into the gloaming of the Conjugal Cabaret. As you cross the portal into this place of potential partnerships, don't get too excited. Note the "No Smoking" sign. We may be using our imaginations here, but let's not tip into the utterly absurd.

The first person you see is a good-looking, take-charge type. Yummy, you think. Introductions are made: "Hi. I'm Aries, but you can call me irresistible." You answer, "Nah, I think I'll call you the one I let get away." Aries shrugs it all off graciously and doesn't seem to care much—for the moment.

Next up is a seductively sturdy type: one who carries the whiff of the Old West and the promise of safety only a six-shooter can provide. Now, this is somebody on whom you can lean. "I'm Taurus," this paragon of security tells you while giving you a firm handshake. Hmmm, you think. You might let him buy you a drink and see where this goes.

"I'd buy you a drink," says Taurus, "but I'm sticking to my budget. I'm also sticking to this bar stool. It's comfortable." After these comments, *you're* uncomfortable, so you trek away from the prairie and into what appears to be a mass of communication devices with a human being in the midst of them.

"Let me introduce myselves. I'm Gemini, the Twins. You are really hot. Just the one I've always been looking for."

"Wow," you think as you take in the youthful appearance and energy of this being. You finally stammer, "Well—er, um, what can I say?" The truth is, you can't say much because the Twins do all the talking.

"Just say you'll sit here and talk only to me. Oops, I've got a call coming in. And gosh, my pager is vibrating. You're my absolute first priority, so I'll get back to you after I've taken these calls."

How can such an obviously quick-witted person fail to see the contradiction here?

You retaliate, "My absolute first priority is to hoof it to somewhere else." Gemini smiles and waves as you experience an unaccountably soothing feeling. Being around such a whirlwind of fruitless activity has left you weary, so you're drawn to that suddenly comforting feeling like a desert traveler to an oasis. The source of this tranquility sits next to an empty bar stool and pats it. Taking this as an invitation, you sit down.

"I'm Cancer," says your host. And true host he is, for surrounding him is an environment so inviting, you'd think he lived there. "You could use a drink. An old fashioned, perhaps?"

How did Cancer know? That's your favorite cocktail. Full of hope and curiosity, you notice how attractive this natural nurturer is and wonder why this is the first time you found nurturing to be so sexy. "Thank you, Cancer, I was getting a bit tired. Tell me about yourself." Cancer replies, "There's really nothing much to tell." (It'd be more accurate to say there's nothing much Cancer *will* tell.) "Why don't you tell me about yourself?" By now, you feel a bit exposed, and suspect your every question will be answered by another question. Taking your drink with you, you try not to feel guilty as you bid Cancer farewell. The downward tug on Cancer's lips cause you to fear you'll need a tugboat to get away from this one.

A little tipsy from your encounters, not to mention the drink, you spy a charismatic, well-dressed person surrounded by lots of people. This is obviously "somebody," and you wonder if you recognize the face from the film you watched last night.

"Where have you been?" booms the Voice of Confidence.

You say, "It looks like you've got your hands full, so . . ."

"Nonsense. I'm Leo, and very glad to meet you. Care to join us?" It's tempting, to be sure, but with that entourage you'll be lucky to get noticed. Besides, there's a bit too much flash here, and it's not coming from cameras—it's light reflecting off of jewelry.

As you slip by Leo calls, "Hey, where are you going?" "Somewhere I won't be asked to account for my movements," you reply.

By now, you need another drink. You belly up to the bar next to a quietly sexy type you'd like to get to know better. "I'm Virgo, and I'm very pleased to meet you. Have a seat, please." There's something compelling about the contrast between the cool exterior and the earthy interior.

"It looks like you're busy, " you say, noticing in Virgo's hand the sleekest Palm Pilot you've ever seen.

"Alas, I am. So many committees and so much to do at work."

"Virgo, what do you do with your spare time?"

The blank look clues you in before Virgo answers, "What's that?"

In the midst of Virgo's confusion, you slip away unnoticed. That's quite a trick, since the Virgin notices everything.

You're becoming a bit confused yourself, so you head for the person who seems to possess the coolest head and best judgment, the eye of the storm of the cabaret. A very smooth voice croons, "How do you do? I am Libra. I couldn't help noticing you seemed a bit confused, if you don't mind my saying so." With that voice, Libra can say anything as far as you're concerned. "Would you like to tell me what's on your mind?"

So you do, keeping to yourself only that the cologne Libra wears makes you forget there's more of the zodiac to explore.

"I do see your point. Taurus is so stunningly stable. On the other hand, there's the problem of persuading the Bull to move. I'm so sorry. I hate to leave you at loose ends, but I have tickets for a play. Shall we meet again?" Yes, if you have any say in the matter.

Suddenly, you feel that someone is staring at you, and knows everything about you. Magnetized, you approach this apparition. You say, "I haven't been around the whole zodiacal block yet, but aren't you Scorpio?" Raising an eyebrow first, this sexy being says, "Yes, I am." Silence.

"Um, I've heard a lot about Scorpio. It was all good." You're fumbling now, afraid anything you say will be held against you in a court of law.

Thankfully, Scorpio pipes in. "Let me give you some advice. I see you've got a letch for Libra. That's cool, but look in your pocket. Gemini lifted your wallet. And while we're on the subject of 'warnings,' look out for Capricorn. Goats look conservative and careful, but they're like sharks. They've got all the sharp teeth and none of the winning personality. See you soon."

Where's the comic relief, you wonder? Fortunately, you don't have to wait long. A floppy-haired poet type takes your hand and says, "Love is not love which alters when it alteration finds or bends with the remover to remove. Oh no, it is an ever-fixed mark that looks upon tempests and is not shaken." Oh, Pisces. Meet the universal soul mate. At this point I, your guide, must intervene.

"Pisces, you jumped ahead in line. Besides, you probably butchered the Bard's sonnet. Go find another mark, and it doesn't have to be ever fixed." Usually docile Pisces walks away muttering something about always being last.

"Why did you banish Pisces? I'd like to experience some of that artistic attitude," you say, looking after Pisces longingly.

"You will," I answer. "He's had one too many martinis tonight. Look, there's the Fish trying to pay a bar tab with his office ID card. Basically, Pisces is okay. Sometimes this Fish acts like a rat, but at least Pisces is a homing rat."

Just then, Sagittarius bounds up to us. "Am I late? Sorry. Who's your friend? And why the long face? Has Scorpio been spooking you? It's just an act. Let me get you a drink. Everything looks better after you enhance your blood supply with a little Guinness." How refreshing, you think. With all that optimism, the Archer must have lots of friends. And off Sadge goes to join them, with a cheery wave goodbye.

There's more. You are about to encounter Capricorn. Unruffled, with an earthy but dignified aura, the Goat stands next to you.

"Allow me to introduce myself. I'm Capricorn. Here's my card. Has Scorpio been jerking your chain?"

"Well, kind of," you answer.

"Were you warned that I'm a barracuda without good manners?" Capricorn inquires.

"Not exactly. But the Scorpion did say Gemini took my wallet."

Cap gasps. "Oh, my God! This is serious indeed. If it had been only your watch, that would've been one thing . . . but don't worry, I'll file the police report." And, laudably, the Goat is as good as his word. Unfortunately, however, there are no police at the Conjugal Cabaret. The bouncer's in charge. What now, you ask yourself?

Now is the word, baby. Aquarius, finally perfecting work on a bona fide time machine, beamed himself into the new century as soon as Woodstock wound down. (That's the first Woodstock, by the way.)

"Cool place. I see our work wasn't in vain. No smoking, though. That doesn't apply to weed, does it? Just kidding. I'm glad to see so many interracial and inter-zodiacal signs can be couples in public."

You are totally intrigued by this highly intelligent being and want to get to know the Water Bearer better. Unfortunately, Aquarius has other plans.

"I'd love to stay, but I'm hopping ahead to see what the rain forests will look like in fifty years. Lush, green, and vaster than ever, if I have anything to say about it! Take it easy."

Now you have met them all. And you've seen some things you like along with some things you definitely don't. What's more, you now know which sign goes with which personality.

sun sign dates

ARIES March 20–April 20

TAURUS April 21–May 21

GEMINI May 22–June 21

CANCER June 22–July 23

LEO July 24–August 23

VIRGO August 24–September 23

LIBRA September 24–October 23

SCORPIO October 24–November 22

SAGITTARIUS November 23–December 21

CAPRICORN December 22–January 20

AQUARIUS January 21–February 19

PISCES February 20–March 19

Note: Sun sign dates are approximate. The exact dates shift around by a day or so, depending on the year.

1 *the enamored egoist*

ARIES—THE RAM, March 20–April 20

ARIES'S INTERNET DATING PROFILE

Q: Favorite movie
A: *Robin Hood*

THE REAL ANSWER: *The Terminator*

Q: Favorite color
A: Red

THE REAL ANSWER: White—as in "white out." It's so easy to get rid of entries in my little black book and write new ones over them.

Q: Favorite book
A: *Treasure Island.* All that adventure is so invigorating.

THE REAL ANSWER: *Tarzan, the Ape Man.* No question who's in charge there.

Q: Favorite classic song

A: "The Impossible Dream." Nothing is impossible, so I play the song over and over for people who don't believe it.

THE REAL ANSWER: "My Way." Put Sinatra's wimpy song in mothballs; listen instead to the Sex Pistols song of the same title.

Q: Favorite drink

A: Super Mega Jolt Cola with ginseng

THE REAL ANSWER: Super Mega Jolt Cola with a triple shot of espresso.

Q: What is your ideal home?

A: Something small that someone else can clean up.

THE REAL ANSWER: Something big that someone else can clean up. Concrete floors are a plus. If I spill anything, all I have to do is hose the place down. Who has time for waxing hardwood floors or vacuuming carpet?

Q: Where will you be in five years?

A: Running a company, and taking over production of the TV series *Survivor.*

THE REAL ANSWER: Living the TV series *Survivor.* It's fun to beat everybody. Especially when they're half naked.

P.S. Aries's posted photograph will be of Aries in action and will, of course, be the best photo you've ever seen.

Getting to Know Aries

Unenlightened people think Aries is besotted only with Aries, and that your presence is required only so the Ram can have group sex (in other words, with Aries, Aries, and you). This is totally untrue. As a lover, those who fall under this sun sign are enamored and decisive. When Aries wants you, you'll know it. The clue won't be sugary words, but definitive action. You will be asked for your phone number and you'll hand it over, or else. Or else what? You'll miss out on being with Aries.

You may feel karma has united you with your true mate. But, at times more reckless than destiny, Aries jumps when the impulse strikes him, especially if said impulse is to jump on someone he finds attractive. This astrological sign is a karmic kamikaze; the Ram doesn't care about consequences in this life, much less consequences in the next.

The Ram is a hero in the traditional definition of the word. This is the classic conqueror: a romantic roustabout with an ardent approach. Much has been made of Aries's need to be first. This is silly. Aries doesn't *need* to be first. Being at the start of the zodiac, the Ram *is* first. And in a relationship, Aries is the first to approach, the first to deliver, and the first to lose interest. Don't take it personally.

If you've met an Aries, you've brushed up against a powerful person. It's no exaggeration to say the Ram is turbocharged—in fact, nuclear powered. It's natural for such a dynamo to take control of any number of things: a corporation, a kitchen, a kennel, or you. *Definitely* you. This tendency can be good when you're between the sheets but if you don't like rolling over on command outside of the sack, watch out.

In light of Aries's straight-shooting communication style, you also can say what's on your mind, right? It's such a relief to avoid the conversational contortionism favored by Pisces and Cancer. Let's see how such direct communication plays out in a fast-forward to pre-dinner prep at home with your very own action hero.

Your Aries says to you as you're unloading the dishwasher, "Hey, just put the plates on the top shelf, the salad bowls on the middle shelf, and the soup bowls on the bottom."

You consider this order of business for a moment while Aries does reconnaissance in the pantry. The soup bowls are used rarely enough that the one on the bottom of the stack has dust around the rim. Aries is so direct, you feel confident enough to say, "Wouldn't it make more sense to put the plates on the bottom shelf? We use them every day, and they'd be within easy reach."

You begin stacking according to plan, knowing Aries gets as excited about expediency as he does about decisive action. Suddenly you can't hear the click of crockery because it's being drowned out by your partner's oratory about why your idea is a bad idea. You thought you'd get to be as straight with Aries as Aries is with you. But instead, you were rewarded with an argument, no dinner, and no sex.

 LESSON If you persist in contradicting Aries's orders, the consequence could be lengthy, belabored instruction.

What's in This Relationship for You

People born under the sign of Aries can be flatteringly ardent. Unfortunately, they're sometimes accused of being flamboyantly arrogant, too. Luckily, only the bad specimens succumb to this personality trait. You're onto a good thing when you and Aries become a team. Read on to discover the upside of relating to the Ram.

Decisiveness

Aries knows what Aries wants, and goes after it no matter what. This is true especially when it comes to romance. What an aphrodisiac! It's exciting to date someone who doesn't need the approval of a focus group of Grandma, coworkers, and ex-significant others before asking you out.

Excitement

Never boring, the Ram can be exasperating, pushy, and romantically mushy. Yet Aries's straightforwardness gives you a feeling of underlying security. It's like riding a satisfyingly scary roller coaster. There are ups and downs, sharp corners, and twists and turns, and you may find yourself flipped upside down, but at least you know that below you, the wheels are attached to a track. That's as comforting as it gets when you're dallying with a daredevil.

How to Attract Aries

Aries is into appearances. This is natural, because when it comes to sex appeal, all Rams are armed and dangerous. You don't necessarily have to be ultra youthful, which is nice to know; some other signs demand romantic candidates just old enough to obtain a driver's license but too young to register to vote. Just be fit, light on your feet, and have a healthy ego. Because Aries does.

Note: If a male Ram says he's a leg man, it doesn't mean you must have beautifully sculpted calves. It means that when things become boring, he'll use his own legs to run away—fast. There are a couple of other ways you can snare Aries, now that you've attracted his or her attention. Or rather, now that Aries has chosen to bestow that attention on lucky you. Read on to find out how subtlety can help you romance the randy Ram.

Act obedient

When Aries tells you it's your turn to mow the lawn, pop right out to the garage to fill up the gas can and rev up the mower. If Aries has a headache and moans, "Oh, will *somebody* get me an aspirin?", run upstairs and open up the Bayer. Don't be put off if your friends start making comments like, "It's wonderful that you're so happy, but don't you think maybe you're bending over backwards just a little too far?" Or maybe a Sagittarius pal says, "You're acting like one of the servants in *Upstairs, Downstairs*. But you don't have an English accent or the cool clothes. Neither does Aries. Did you know that that TV program had more viewers than . . . ."

Be sure to interrupt Sadge before you are subjected to a discourse on the history of *Masterpiece Theatre*. You can smile to yourself because you know obedience is merely Phase One. Now it's time to introduce you to Phase Two.

Be disobedient

Aries has had a rotten day. The boss rebuked the Ram in front of underlings. On such occasions, you're usually there to soothe with aromatherapy candles, lavender massage oil, and ready and nimble fingers. Your conversation should go something like this:

ARIES "It would be great to get one of your massages. I'm ready."

YOU "There's nothing I'd love to do more. But I can't. I have dinner plans."

ARIES (*who's hurting because of muscular tension and your "insensitivity"*) "What? Then cancel them."

YOU "Can't do it, hon. You wouldn't like it if I canceled our Saturday round of golf."

ARIES "But this is d—"

YOU "No, it's not different. I'll see you after dinner. And since I know you love a good curry, I'll even let you have my doggie bag. Bye!"

It's too bad you won't be there to see it, but Aries is stupefied. Shocked. Out of kilter. And absolutely fascinated—by you. Why? You were getting a little too boringly devoted for Aries's taste, and now you've changed.

Well, actually, *you* haven't changed—your *tactics* have changed.

 LESSON Aries has contradictory, even hypocritical, desires when it comes to love and relationships.

Rams want unconditional devotion, yet don't respect someone who makes them the center of their universe. Aries can't stand being contradicted, but at the same time loves a good quarrel. Does this mean the Ram needs two different people to satisfy these conflicting desires? Not necessarily. However, it does mean you have to deal with these conflicting desires. Yes, it's exhausting at times—but never dull.

The Aries Deal Breaker: Indolence

Aries is on the move so much that usually only a Gemini (or another Aries) can keep up. If you want to spend too much time on the couch watching *Six Feet Under*, that's exactly where your relationship will end up.

The Committed Relationship: You Got What You Wanted; Now Here's How to Keep It

Holding onto an Aries is tricky. One problem that will rear its ugly head concerns who is to be in charge. Here's a suggestion that can help you tackle that issue: Take charge when Aries can't see you doing it.

Aries does it Aries's way. Maybe the two of you have decided to acquire property. Let's imagine you openly take control. You call the real estate agent, a contractor, and a title research company. If you do all of this without Aries's approval or input and get away with it with furniture and dishes intact, expect a call from the Nobel committee in Sweden commending you for keeping the peace between Aries's inclinations and his actions.

LESSON Manipulate by taking charge when the Ram is out of sight, of the house, or even of the country.

Hold on to your own personality

It's imperative that you keep your identity. One saying contends that if you rub against gold for long enough, some of it may rub off on you. There's truth to this rustic little phrase. You like your style, but sincerely admire some of Aries's qualities. Maybe a few will rub off, enhance your personality, and help transform you into an upgraded version of yourself. Maybe so, but it will take a DNA-compatible asbestos suit to hang onto your own persona around someone with such heat-tempered strength.

 LESSON Keep strong ties to the life you had before Aries. Otherwise you'll end up in an unreleased Marx brothers film tentatively titled *A Night at the Asylum.*

Persuade Aries to slow down

The important word here is "persuade." You and Aries have been so busy with projects and activities that you've spent two months' worth of weekends apart. This weekend, you plan to attend a concert and go salsa dancing afterwards. Sure, it took some arm-twisting for Aries to agree to sit still for an entire concert—that, and the promise of dancing. As you place the concert tickets on a table near the front door, you notice Aries dragging out the gym bag and filling it with bottled water, an extra T-shirt, spare running-shoe laces, and other items that spark your suspicions.

YOU "Why are you packing your bag now? You usually do it before you go for a long run. And at the last minute."

ARIES "I do not. Remember our trip to Bali? I packed an entire hour before the airport shuttle came to pick us up."

YOU "Forget Bali. What about the bag?"

ARIES "You know this weekend's marathon run that's being held downtown? I promised I'd participate."

YOU "Promised whom?"

Aries names a pal and competitor who once said, "Aries, you're a sprinter. The day you run a marathon is the day Paris Hilton does her own nails."

YOU "You can run anytime. Run to your heart's content—or collapse—during the week. Tonight, we've got a date."

Aries pontificates about the fact that the marathon benefits charity. It's obvious it benefits Aries's penchant for panting his way around a track or city block. Besides, for the Ram it's so boring to sit still.

Don't expect Aries to back down without a fight. Here's your chance to be devious.

YOU "Now I get it. You're going to run a marathon just because someone said you can't."

(This may be a factor, but it's actually got more to do with Arian restlessness than anything else.) Aries doesn't want anyone to think he can be goaded into doing anything. Try to be gracious, and allow your Aries to save face.

> **YOU** "I don't know what got into me. You wouldn't let some silly competitive comment make you break our date."
>
> **ARIES** "Of course I wouldn't. Spending time with you is more important than a marathon."

Give your Ram a grateful hug. But watch the fridge. In order to curb that characteristic Arian restlessness, carefully monitor all products that contain caffeine. God knows Aries has more than enough natural get-up-and-go. You might even do something really evil, like mix decaffeinated coffee beans with the full strength variety. Aries will become calmer, less likely to undergo cardiac arrest, and you won't have to give so many tension-related massages.

Do's and Don'ts in the Aries Mating Game

Do be introspective. The Ram is short on introspection, so this is an area in which you can have an advantage.

Do be a graceless loser. Remember, Aries likes winners.

Don't expect consistency. Aries is showing signs of restlessness. Maybe he or she murmured someone else's name while you were making love. Before you reach for a knife, remember you can use this

lapse to pounce on Aries when he shows signs of jealousy. Wait . . .
Aries, jealous? Confident, swaggering Aries gets jealous? Absolutely.

Don't be complacent. With all this direct action and speech, you
may think that everything's great between the both of you. Otherwise the Ram would speak up, right? Not necessarily: the Ram can
be cunning. Yes, the intense-but-restless Aries sometimes experiences the itch to explore. Conquest is part of the fun in life for Aries.
Your fun is the revenge you can take if the Ram goes too far.

You Want Out: Ways to Leave Your Loser

Aries men and women have a lot of pride, so just telling them to go
away will do the trick. But neither you (nor most people) are callous
enough to end the relationship, unless Aries has committed unforgivable deeds, like writing checks against your checking account,
sleeping with one of your siblings, or submitting a nude photo of you
to the producers of HBO's *Real Sex.*

Chances are, though, you won't get the opportunity to do the
ditching. Aries often loses interest first, so be prepared for the even-
tuality by thinking of fifteen gracious ways of accepting—or even
celebrating—life without Aries.

Bliss or Bloodshed: How Your Sign Fits with Aries

♈ ♈ *Aries with Aries* An Aries paired with another Aries can be
like an action film in which the heroes triumph, or the entire world

ends by blowing up. It depends on how cooperative you will be with each other. On the upside, you both enjoy being active; there will be few major disagreements about keeping busy. Also the sexual attraction will be immediate, and you'll have fun in bed (and on the kitchen table and back seat of your car). On the other hand, arguments will take place, and one of you must back down or the relationship will back up like a clogged sink. While both of you Rams are quick to come to the rescue, few like to clean up messes. Concede every once in a while, and you can have a lifetime of fun. The alternative is to blow up your world. It's up to you.

♉♈ **Taurus with Aries** As a Taurus, you can be grounding to an Aries; even the Ram gets tired of being revved up all the time. You're less likely to become rattled or rise to the bait when Aries expresses irritation, an equanimity that is good for your health. But, keep in mind that while your composure is discouraging to Aries's desire to get a rise out of you, the Ram actually appreciates a worthy opponent—or at least one who reacts. Some Rams don't realize that Bulls spar in a different way. Aries trots about, flicking light punches at an opponent. Taurus hits once, and it's a knockout. Relationship over. Have dialogue about your different styles and adapt to them, or you'll be in trouble. Another potential problem is that unlike many Rams, Bulls can be homebodies. This disparity, however, can make for a healthier relationship. When Aries has a partner's approval to have an active social life, Taurus can enjoy some alone time. Be sure to talk your differences over first, though, or Arians will feel unappreciated, and Bulls will feel excluded.

♊ ♈ **Gemini with Aries** Both Aries and Gemini appreciate speed. Aries, it's your approach to life's challenges; Gem, it's your approach to love affairs. As a result, it's possible for you two to wear each other out. While this may be amusing for your friends to watch, it's no fun to experience. Yet for Gemini, dealing with someone who's straightforward can be refreshing. Maybe Aries possesses traits you don't like, but at least he or she doesn't try to conceal them. Sometimes the Twins' indirect nature is the serpent that slithers through the Aries/Gemini Garden of Eden. This charming, witty asset to any party or psych ward can sometimes seem like a different person. Aries, try not to be too hard on this Renaissance romantic. Dr. Jekyll didn't remember what he did while hiding behind Hyde. Not at first, anyway.

♋ ♈ **Cancer with Aries** Crabs have a reputation for being nurturing and caring individuals. That's okay, because you are. But that's not all you are—you're also leaders. Arians tend to disregard your leadership traits, and choose instead to believe that they have a pliable, complacent little worshipper at their side. This misconception will disappear the moment you two cohabitate, if not before. And Aries, if it doesn't hit you right away, look around you. Where is your house? In the neighborhood Cancer prefers. How is it decorated? The way Cancer envisioned. Before you feel you've been tricked, remember how those choices were made. The first home you looked at was in the part of town you preferred. And the first decorator was recommended by you. Cancer, who consulted you at each stage, has gotten—not through magic, but as a result of great effort—what he or she wanted without stepping on your Arian toes or injuring your pride. This revelation gives you an insight into the Cancer/Aries relationship. Cancer, will you always get your own way? No, but if you and Aries stay together, the Ram will discover what it's like to compromise. Not a bad lesson for the Ram to learn, even if learning it is achieved while sitting on a chair that didn't seem appealing even in the showroom.

♌ ♈ **Leo with Aries** Leos are attracted to Rams the way actors are to red carpets. And, the attraction is mutual. You're both sparkling personalities who like to see, be seen, and especially be seen conspicuously consuming. Aries, you'll be proud of your Lion—a pride that is reciprocated. The troubles created by this pairing are usually avoided when it's a romantic relationship. Otherwise, Leo and Aries will constantly try to one-up each other. There will be some fights in the bathroom over mirror time, but you can work out a schedule. Be sure to provide plenty of room for stowing your hairstyling products, fragrances, and lotions. Especially the lotions: both of you enjoy massages. When an Aries and Leo hook up for a one-on-one massage session, it should stay private. Okay, private except for your sex cam.

♍ ♈ **Virgo with Aries** Someone once said Virgos are prudes with few sexual desires—but this someone has obviously never dated one. Virgos are sexually earthy, and they're particular, too. So, Aries, if Virgo has chosen you, feel flattered. And enjoy lounging on Virgo's beautiful sheets. You'll wake up to the smell of gourmet coffee and think, "Relationships just don't get any better than this." In the kitchen, undoubtedly your favorite newspaper is waiting in pristine condition. You assume the voluptuous Virgo must be in the bathroom. Then you notice a note:

"Dear Aries, What a lovely evening we had. I'm at the office, but I set a timer before I left so fresh coffee would be waiting for you when you get out of bed. I can't wait to see you tonight.

P.S. Would you please toss the sheets in the washer before you go? And please don't forget to lock up and set the alarm before you leave."

You start to panic, then notice it's still dark outside. Virgo arrives at the office early—very early. And works very late. So, learn to live with it, or live without Virgo.

♎ ♈ **Libra with Aries** Libras love romance and all its trappings. At first, Aries's certainty that you're The One lures you. Sooner or later, your differences will surface and Aries will feel trapped. Aries's fire burns itself out. The romancing techniques will go up in flames, too. You thought you'd always continue to receive the unexpected card, or a bunch of balloons would be delivered to your office— gestures that were made liberally during the conquest phase. You didn't really expect Aries to keep it up, did you? (Well, yes. Most of the other signs would, too.) Aries and Libra are opposites on the zodiacal wheel. This usually means you'll be attracted to each other sexually, but you may not be as well suited once you put your clothes on. Much depends on which other signs influence your individual horoscopes. One thing, Ram, is certain: Libras look for a partner. Aries, if you're still into the conquering game, approach Libra when you're ready to settle down.

♏ ♈ **Scorpio with Aries** It's often said that there's more to a successful relationship than sex. This statement wasn't made by a Scorpio or an Aries, though. Oddly enough, a match between these two signs can work. Both of you understand passion, although Scorpio is better at keeping it alive longer. If anyone can keep an Aries interested in the long term, it's a Scorpio. How can this be, with two such controlling individuals? Scorpios don't mind letting Aries take the dominant role—on the surface, that is. But Aries, you will object to Scorpio's subtle, cunning ways. Also, both of you will need to keep the jealousy under control. Or don't, and use it as an excuse for having lots of make-up sex.

♐ ♈ **Sagittarius with Aries** Sagittarians and Arians get along well. Sagittarians can shrug off the Ram's controlling ways better than most signs. But can Rams overlook Sadge's occasional tactless comment? Probably, as long as the barb doesn't hit one of Aries's soft spots. (Sensitive areas include the Ram's looks, accomplishments, and income tax bracket.) Sadge honestly doesn't mean to offend. So Aries, don't get into a dust-up about it. And Sadge, realize that just because the Ram is strong, it doesn't mean he or she lacks feelings. Other than these potential pitfalls, you two can have a great romance and fulfilling love life.

♑ ♈ **Capricorn with Aries** To Capricorn, sexual sizzle is nice but a six-figure income is better. By contrast, although you Arians have healthy respect for cash and all the great toys it can buy, in romance buff bodies and sexual fireworks take precedence, and dollar signs follow. Both of you like to be respected and looked up to by the other. Settle for appreciating your common strengths and different approaches. Capricorn, you're more subdued (outwardly, at least) and sometimes cringe when Aries is bounding through a room with all that bonhomie. Live with it. Aries, you may view the Goat as boring on occasion. Encourage the Goat to have fun the Aries way, but remember you're up against a strong personality that won't fold just because you push against it. Once you realize this, you'll be more patient and Cap will have a better time. What a transformation!

♒ ♈ **Aquarius with Aries** Aquarians like Aries's decisiveness and courage to attempt the impossible. The Aries openness is refreshing, but not when it goes to extremes. And you, Rams, don't get it when the Water Bearer shushes your chatter about Aquarius's personal life. After all, privacy is a Scorpio thing and here we're talking about Aquarius. As Aries, you're no Sadge when it comes to tactlessness, so what's the big deal? This is the big deal: Aquarians like privacy when it comes to certain personal issues. Yes, they're open, but this openness also includes the idea of abolishing social security numbers and background checks. Why would the free speech–loving and tech fetishist Water Bearer be so deeply private? Aries, before you call Aquarius a hypocrite, consider the reason. To Aquarius, the weird and wonderful world of technology opens up many other worlds. Unfortunately, one of those resembles the world that George Orwell described in *1984*. This is one thing that inspires fear in Aquarius. Try to relate by contemplating your own fears. Okay, well, make some up if you don't have any, and you and Aquarius will have fun running around together.

♓ ♈ **Pisces with Aries** Pisces, you are the maestro of misdirection, and if there's anything that angers an Aries, it's bad directions of any kind. Actually, the problem with this combination is that you Arians are natural dominators, and Pisceans are easily dominated—or so it seems. Pisces, you'll relax for a while, happy to let Aries take charge of making decisions about everything, from ordering subscriptions to lifestyle magazines, up to and including the kind of car you should buy. Then, when Aries continues this pattern, you'll begin to feel stifled, pinned down, and suffocated. You'll start doing things your own way: in private. Unfortunately, Aries views this as sneakiness. What happens then? More controlling behavior from Aries and more silent rebellion from you. The best way to handle this issue is for you to vocalize your discontent, Pisces. And Aries, though you're justly famous for your strength, for you much-needed empathy takes work. Make the effort to put yourself in Pisces's position. And when you do, you'll understand how Pisces feels. There's never a question that you'll take action when it is necessary to do so. Now that you truly understand the best steps to take, you and Pisces can find balance in your emotional domination and submission areas. Then you can use what you've learned in the bedroom, where you can really have some fun with it.

the bullheaded hedonist

TAURUS—THE BULL, April 21–May 21

 TAURUS'S INTERNET DATING PROFILE

Q: Favorite movie
A: *Dr. Zhivago*

THE REAL ANSWER: *Dances with Wolves*, watched while cuddling up to an extra-large tub of salty, buttery popcorn. Actually, as long as I can spend four hours with my feet up and my favorite snack, I don't really care what the hell I'm watching.

Q: Favorite book
A: *Underworld* by Don DeLillo

THE REAL ANSWER: *Tristram Shandy* by Laurence Sterne. All that circuitous eighteenth-century lingo takes absolutely forever to plow through. Isn't it great?

Q: Favorite song
A: "Slow Train Comin'" by Bob Dylan

THE REAL ANSWER: "Slow Train Comin'" by Bob Dylan. Don't even bother asking me to speed up, because I'm not able—or willing.

Q: Favorite drink
A: Jameson 1780, the best aged whiskey money can buy.

THE REAL ANSWER: Jameson 1780, stirred into a nice, relaxing cup of tea, enjoyed from the comfort of my leather sofa. No Cosmopolitans or chocolate martinis for me; I never understood the whole cocktail-craze thing. Kids these days—mm.

Q: What is your ideal home?
A: A restored nineteenth-century mansion, complete with pantry, servant's quarters, drawing room, and wine cellar.

THE REAL ANSWER: A restored nineteenth-century mansion, complete with home entertainment system and separate quarters for my DVD collection.

Q: Where will you be in five years?
A: Five years into the fourteenth draft of my first novel (estimated length: at least 600 pages).

THE REAL ANSWER: The same place I am now: on the couch.

Getting to Know Taurus

You've just finished a fling with a flighty Sagittarius, and boy, are you tired. All that transcontinental travel; flitting from party to party on Friday nights; and the endless weekend hiking trips, skiing trips, whitewater rafting trips, sailing trips—not to mention the whirlwind of Sadge's exes you've met, because now they're his best friends. "Honey, you remember Sarah (or Anya, Louise, Nanette, Shauna), don't you?" Well, no, you don't. Who can blame you? You're exhausted. You can't remember the last time you actually spent a night *in*.

This is the reason why the Taurus you're seeing now is so refreshing, so relaxing. Taurus doesn't want to drag you out club hopping on Thursdays (you have to work the next morning, after all), and isn't insistent that you spend your next vacation scaling the Grand Canyon (with one hand tied behind your back). Taurus actually wants to cuddle, the both of you whiling away long winter nights curled up on the couch in front of a fire, watching a stack of old movies. Thank heavens the Bull can sit still long enough to enjoy a week at the beach sipping specialty drinks and doing absolutely nothing. It's like dating a Scorpio without the mood swings. *Ahh*, you think to yourself, this is the life.

Yes, it is . . . well, one sort of life. Taurus, the Bull, may be the steadiest sign in the zodiac. Remember that old adage about the tortoise and the hare? That describes the Bull in a nutshell—sometimes, slow and steady really does win the race. You won't find too many Taureans whose career goal is to be President of the United

States, the next winner on *American Idol*, or CEO of a high-powered brokerage firm.

But remind yourself that those highs you hungered for—and experienced—when you were seeing Sadge or Gemini were accompanied by real lows. With Taurus, you won't have to worry about that (although you might sometimes wish you did). Loyal and reliable to a fault, Taurus remembers birthdays, pays her bills on time, picks up the kids at 5 P.M. sharp, and never forgets to put out the recycling on Tuesday mornings.

And Taurus will never, ever cheat.

All this sounds like the recipe for big time success. But wait a minute. This is life, not *It's A Wonderful Life*. The downside of Bulls is that actually getting them to *do* anything can be extremely enervating. Trying to pry a Taurus off the couch, out of his routine, and into a spontaneous mode may, more likely than not, be a Sisyphean task like that guy in Greek mythology who spent eternity trying to roll a boulder up a mountain—only to have it slip from his hands and roll right back down just as it's about to reach the peak. Don't let Tortoise—er, Taurus's—inertia get to you. Just remember that you're going to have to be the catalyst for action in this relationship, the proverbial hare.

Let's pretend it's the middle of December, and the holidays are just around the corner. You've always loved New Year's Eve, and this year your best friend is throwing a party. You're psyched: you and Taurus haven't gone out in ages (well, you did venture out to the movies once, in October). After a successful four-hour shopping expedition to find the perfect festive-yet-chic dress, you hop downstairs to show your new little red number to Taurus.

YOU (STRUTTING YOUR STUFF) Look at this, honey! I got it on sale, and it's going to be great for Emily's New Year's party.

TAURUS (UNGLUING HIS EYES FROM *THE SHAWSHANK REDEMPTION* AND CROSSING HIS SWEATPANT-CLAD LEGS ON THE COFFEE TABLE) Party? New Year's?

YOU (DOING A LITTLE SHIMMY) Of course. Doesn't this make my derriere look great?

TAURUS So we're really going to that, huh?

YOU We RSVP'ed a month ago. We're going.

TAURUS Oh. Okay. I thought we could stay home. You know, order in Chinese, open that bottle of Barolo we've been saving. . . .

YOU (UNMOVED EVEN BY THE MENTION OF YOUR FAVORITE RED WINE) We're *going*. Did I tell you Emily ordered a whole case of Piper Heidsieck for the party?

TAURUS (HORNS SUDDENLY PERKING UP) Piper Heidsieck? The champagne of the gods! Let's bring dessert.

Here's a hint: mention fine edibles. It may come as a surprise, considering the Bull's stolid and stoic nature, but Taureans love all things Epicurean. The promise of a gourmet dinner or fine wine will have your partner hoofing it out the door by your side.

What's the moral of the story? Be persistent. It's not that the Bull doesn't want to go to that party, or to Los Angeles to visit your brother, or hot-air ballooning; he just needs to be *reminded* that he wants to go. And that the destination merits leaving the couch.

What's in This Relationship for You

Taureans are known for going the distance. When dating a Bull, you won't enjoy (or suffer from) any Arian- or Sagittarian-style bursts of energy, or the accompanying emotional rush that so often accompanies them. But if you're not the roller-coaster type, that could be a good thing. Read on to find out more.

Steadfastness

Unlike Aries, who only ran that marathon because someone insisted he couldn't, the Bull is known for going the distance. Taurus does not screw around, literally or figuratively. When he's dating you, he's dating you, and that's it. So you can rest assured that when he says he's spending the weekend with his sister in Boston, he really is, and when he tells you he's working late to finish a grant proposal for tomorrow's meeting, he is indeed plugging away at facts and figures at his desk, oblivious to the sexy secretary working late alongside him. Taurus is honest—pure and simple—and he expects you to be, too.

Luckily for those of us who were born under more volatile signs, the earthy Bull is not easily spooked or rattled by his partner's moods. It's his nature to take things in stride. Let's say you've just gotten home from work after one of Those Days. Your computer crashed, your assistant came down with the flu and went home early, lunch was spent fighting the crowds at Bloomingdale's to return those pants you never should have bought anyway, and on your way back to the office, a bird mistook the pants you're currently wearing for a target. (Now you'd kill for those just-returned pants.) It's almost 8 P.M. and it's your turn to cook. Dinner won't be ready for another hour at this rate. You're banging pots and pans and muttering profanities under your breath. Does the Bull stamp and snort and complain that he's hungry, and ask why the hell you're in such a snit anyway? No. Silently, he reaches for the paper towels and cleans as you cook, so you won't have to later. He also discreetly opens a bottle of good Chardonnay.

Stamina

Taurus goes for what he wants, no matter how long it takes. He'll keep going, and going, and going. When what he wants is you, you can sit back and reap the benefits, including inside the bedroom. Don't worry about the wham-bam-thank-you-ma'am kind of nookie. Taureans enjoy quality sex, and they prefer it prolonged, intense, and often. Here is where a Taurus's inertia can work to your advantage. Unplug the alarm clock and stick your cell phone under the mattress, because you're going to be otherwise engaged for quite a while. Like all earth signs, Bulls are sensual and touch oriented—a drive that stems from the same source as their love of fine food and drink—so yours will be happy to spend long hours treating you to a shiatsu massage, nibbling Belgian chocolate from your belly button, and running his hands over your sensitive spots. And the best part is, he'll remember what gets you especially revved up, for next time.

How to Attract Taurus

Believe me, waving a red tablecloth in front of Taurus's face and yelling "Toro!" is *not* the way to go. Or perhaps it is—if you want the Bull to go charging away from you. True to the animal after which their sign is named, Bulls are unnerved and flustered by lots of wiggling, giggling, and distracting, bright colors. What does this mean if you're trying to seduce a Taurus? It doesn't imply you need to be a shrinking violet or that you shouldn't try to look and feel your sexiest. It means you need to strike a very fine balance between assertive and understated when it comes to your come-on—and your appearance.

Quality, not quantity (or lack thereof)

Keep in mind that Taureans like the good life. They'll be attracted to partners who value substance over style. For women, this means more Gwyneth Paltrow than Paris Hilton. On a first date, look appropriate for the occasion. That is, don't over- or underdress. If you're meeting him at a café, followed by a stroll around town and perhaps a movie, wear a white T-shirt, your favorite presentable jeans, and stylish brown boots. Make sure the T-shirt is well made, cut perfectly to your figure, and flattering but not overly revealing. The jeans must be clean, ironed, and well-fitting (but they're too tight if you can't stick both hands into the waistband). Designer labels are chic but not absolutely necessary. The boots should be leather, with a modest heel. Yes, particulars are important to Taurus. Show that you care about your appearance, although it doesn't occupy your every waking moment. If you're making an appearance at a party, whether Taurus is your date or you're trying to catch his fancy, keep these three words in mind: Little Black Dress.

Why dress stylishly and flatteringly, without being too seductive? Taurus, the persistent Bull, likes to see his hard work pay off.

If you show him what he wants to see right away, he's going to miss out on the fun of the chase.

Have specific interests

Who doesn't value intelligence and depth of character in his or her partner (well, maybe Gemini)? Taureans certainly do. But remember, Bulls are super focused. Relatively serious, they tend to pursue their goals and interests relentlessly. Show that you're secure enough to be enthusiastic about their achievements. Say you run into a sexy Bull at a cocktail party. Your conversation should *not* go something like this:

YOU Hey, baby. Come here often?

TAURUS Um.

YOU So what do you do for a living? I bet you're running for President. President of the Hotties Club, that is! Ever been parasailing? I did it a few times, before I got into deep-sea diving, triathlons, and the Book of the Month Club. Man, was that great. Of course, it doesn't hold a candle to steeplechase. You know, I used to be a jockey. . . .

It should sound more like this:

YOU So, I hear you're a friend of Joanne's. You met her in that watercolor class she was taking, right?

TAURUS (INTRIGUED THAT YOU'VE DONE YOUR RESEARCH) Right. I've been painting for years, but thought I'd take a refresher class.

YOU Hey, impressive. I've done a few sketches in charcoal when I've had the chance, ever since I took a mixed-media class back in college. What do you think of Georgia O'Keeffe's work?

The point here isn't that you have to have precisely the same interests. Instead, enjoy your own long-time pursuits at the same time as you're supportive of *her* activities (activities which will be long-term interests by default; after all, she's a Taurus). Sure, when a Taurus focuses her intense, determined attention on you, it feels great. But her energy will be absorbed by other areas of her life as well, so you'll also want to have other activities to turn to.

Be introspective yet extroverted

You want to be able to draw Taurus away from his mental armchair and into your arms. But whatever you do, don't take on a "bubbly" affect. Avoid the "I'm-a-bouncy-Barbie" shtick. That may work for some signs, but Taurus demands authenticity, and falseness (and fals*ies*, for that matter) will turn him off. Furthermore, he'll become ill at ease, and retreat once again into his armchair-*cum*-armor.

The idea with Taurus—and this is a good rule of thumb when you're getting to know any sign, but it's particularly important when that sign is the Bull—is to be only the most genuinely gregarious version of yourself, since you'll have to tease Taurus out of his shell. Ask him questions about himself—*smart* questions. Don't just nod and smile, or the conversation will fizzle out quickly. Make and hold eye contact, and encourage subtle physical contact without being overtly sexual. You can lay your hand on his arm and fix him with a thoughtful glance, saying, "I'm just going to grab some more of that addictive foie gras and another glass of wine. Can I get you the same?" Not only are you showing genuine, affectionate interest in Taurus, you're offering to bring him food, leaving open the potential for love at first bite.

The Taurus Deal Breaker: Nagging

Okay, so it's true that in any relationship, both partners are going to bug each other about leaving the toilet seat up, straightening the kitchen right after dinner instead of first thing in the morning; and using each other's razors in a pinch. To a certain extent, such exchanges are healthy; and can actually be an impetus to get chores done. But when it comes to the Bull, a little goes a long way. Taureans are persistent to a fault, and they admire perseverance in others—and yes, it takes a lot to irritate them. But when you persevere in nagging, that's another story. Drop by drop, like Chinese water torture, the nagging seeps into the Bull's consciousness, and then boy, does he see red. Remind your Taurus about little things gently and tenderly, and give him plenty of positive reinforcement when he responds.

The Committed Relationship: You Got What You Wanted; Here's How to Keep It

Be indulgent

Indulge Taurus in his love for the good things in life, even if you may have more spartan tastes. (Since Taureans are usually careful accountants and planners, they'll probably have sufficient money for some luxuries.) Let him enjoy some extras, and don't resent him for doing so. Say the kitchen floor needs retiling. It's going to cost a couple of thousand bucks, and Taurus's latest freelance writing project hasn't borne fruit yet. Unexpectedly, Taurus books a daylong massage, facial, and hot-stone treatment at the priciest spa in town. You're irked—you haven't been out on the town in the last six weeks and you've made a point of picking up overtime at work whenever you could get it. What gives? Is Taurus saying he expects you to float Project Kitchen Floor? No, this is simply Taurean stress relief. Trust the Bull. He's always got one eye on the books, even when he's treating himself. Compromise a little, and you'll soon know that Taurus rarely lets anyone down.

Indulge your Bull, too, in his need for lots of time alone. It's easy for more gregarious signs to misinterpret this yen for solitude as rejection. But that's the furthest thing from the truth. Taurus simply needs his space—in the best possible way. He doesn't want a lot of frenetic energy humming around him at all times. Look at the upside: Taurus certainly won't take it the wrong way when you want to have a friends-*sans*-significant-other night on the town.

 LESSON Taureans are deeply attuned to their own physical and emotional needs. Trust them, even if it's difficult—and sometimes it *will* be tough.

Be patient

Those two little words mean oh so much. Again, Taurus's plodding, methodical style can be maddening—even to other Taureans who have a bit more get-up-and-go. You might want to scoop his eyes out with a slotted spoon, but hold back. The worst thing you can do is blow up at him.

Remember that being with a Taurus is a long-term investment; patience yields high dividends.

 LESSON Patience is a virtue. If you're a Type-A personality and dating a Taurean, do your best to stay calm and remember Grandma's favorite adage: Haste makes waste. When doing that fails to soothe you, take up Zen meditation.

Be graciously receptive

Let your Bull do things for you. Taureans are motivated to work toward goals, and love to see them achieved. And of course, they reach their goals at their own pace. Sit back and relax, and fight the urge to attempt to speed up the process. As intently as if he were planning a wedding, Taurus will begin arranging an August getaway for the two of you in January. All he's telling you is, it'll be a romantic weeklong escape—the rest is a surprise until he works out all the details. But your sister *is* getting married in August, and you're the maid of honor. How are you supposed to make plans of your own, to *live*, for the next few months while the Bull snorts—I mean, sorts—everything out?

Relax; Taurus is organizing things way, *waaaay* ahead of time precisely so he won't run into any snafus with your schedule and his—and he won't. Whatever you do, don't seem ungrateful. If you do, you'll never hear the end of it.

LESSON A Taurus who loves you will want to treat you like gold. So what if he's actually making the gold himself, out of a few chunks of lead in an alchemist's lab? Meddling and nagging won't get you anywhere with your Bull. Learn to wait, and when Taurus presents you with a tour-de-force treat, reward him with profuse thanks and lots of good, earthy, old-fashioned shagging.

Do's and Don'ts in the Taurus Mating Game

Here are a few tips that should keep your relationship from impaling itself on a pair of very, very sharp horns.

Do use positive reinforcement. Despite the Bull's steady-wins-the-race stoicism, Taureans tend to have very tender hearts that need constant validation.

Do show gratitude, especially for the little things. When he comes home from the drugstore with a box of lavender-scented Kleenex ($3.99) when all you asked for was the fifty-nice cent store brand, don't grumble about money. What he's saying is, I want to pamper you. What should you say in response? "Thank you."

Do tune in to their moods. It won't be hard, because their moods will be pretty visible. If she's painting in her studio, leave her there till she's ready to come in. Don't insist that she come back to the kitchen to help with dinner. Bring her a cup of hot chocolate, and suggest ordering in tonight.

Do get her off the couch, literally or figuratively, using gentle nudges. A little of the above-mentioned positive reinforcement should do the trick. Want to get your Taurus to try skydiving? Lure her with the promise of something sensuous and relaxing afterward—like a daylong wine tasting, a concert, or just a long evening *à deux*, accompanied by chocolate sauce and specialty condoms. She'll love you doubly for it.

Do touch them. Bulls are very physical, and love to be cuddled and petted. During dinner at his parents, keep one hand on his thigh under the tablecloth; hold hands while you're watching TV.

Don't be overly snarky or belligerent. Taureans are rarely sarcastic; they don't respond well to taunting, even if it's meant in good fun.

Don't move her cheese. That is, don't change her physical environment around a great deal without consulting her. Coming home to find the bedroom furniture rearranged, for example, will only confuse her and throw her off balance.

Don't be excessively excessive. Do not show up at his house blitzed on booze or any other type of mood enhancer or depressant. There's a good chance you'll be bouncing off the walls (with either energy or drunkenness), and a hyped-up partner will freak Taurus out.

Don't micromanage. No one likes to be micromanaged, *especially* Taurus. Doing so is a surefire way to get nowhere fast.

You Want Out: Ways to Leave Your Loser

When push finally came to shove, you couldn't get your Bull to budge. You've had enough of Taurus's pigheaded obstinacy (which you used to call "admirable persistence"), and you want out, *now*. So how?

- Wear a turquoise vinyl miniskirt to his company holiday party and chatter to his boss about the latest Britney album.
- Take her bungee jumping, and don't tell her where you're going until you get there. Then, when she hesitates at the edge of the platform, push her.
- Become a barfly. Arrive home no earlier than 3 A.M. every night. (At first he won't mind having the house to himself, but your showing up in an altered state will soon wear on him.) Be sure to reek of cheap bourbon, and to pass out immediately.
- Stop saying "please" and "thank you."
- Don't just ask him to clean out the garage. Ask him, then tell him; next, leave him a voice mail about it at the office, send him a text message, and leave a note on the refrigerator. Finally, call his mother, and ask her to remind him.

Bliss or Bloodshed: How Your Sign Fits with Taurus

♈♉ **Aries with Taurus** See Chapter 1, Taurus with Aries.

♉♉ **Taurus with Taurus** Are two Bulls better than one? Sometimes. Here's the upside. Each of you will understand and respect the other's need for physical and emotional space, and you're so alike in your slow-and-steady-wins-the-race attitudes that chances are you won't get on each other's nerves. It'll be a nice, comfortable, steady relationship—and to be sure, two Taureans in love aren't likely to fight over the major, life-changing stuff. They'll be much more apt to sweat the small stuff, though, like whose turn it is to rule the remote control—or whose rear end it was that caused that huge indentation in the couch. After all, the two of you are going to be spending a lot of time on it. If you're a Taurus who's seeking a long-term mate, great. But if you're looking to sow your proverbial wild oats, look further than a fellow Bull for a bit of fun.

♊ ♉ **Gemini with Taurus** Ever tried to confuse your pet cat? It's easy. Dangle a colorful ball of string—or an edible treat—in front of Fluffy, then jerk it back and forth till it's moving too fast for her to see. Gemini will do the same thing to Taurus—verbally. Fluffy enjoys the game, but Taurus won't be able to keep up, either with Gem's endless, capricious chatter or her yen for constant change and boundless variety. Staid Taurus will seem desperately boring and inert by comparison. Gem might be a good transition lover for Taurus—think "starter marriage," but ultimately, Taurus won't keep her amused for long.

♋ ♉ **Cancer with Taurus** The only strife in this relationship will be over who's the cuddler and who's the one being cuddled? Cancer and Taurus are both very nurturing, loyal signs. And there won't be any tugs-of-war à la the Taurus/Gemini match, since both Bull and Crab move very, very slowly. That means that the two will work toward financial stability together; they'll believe that their home is truly their castle; and not a single rash, thoughtless decision will shake their foundation. What *will* shake them? Well, they even share a weak point: insecurity. If a Cancer feels unloved, he can tend to act irrationally, for instance, going off to pinch the behind of a cute Virgo. When a Taurus has been betrayed, or suspects she *might* have been betrayed, the relationship's as good as over. If Cancer and Taurus actually show each other their tender underbellies, though, this duo has true long-term potential.

♌♉ *Leo with Taurus* At first glance, it may seem that these two are about as compatible as sour-cream-and-onion potato chips with a milk-chocolate-bar chaser. But don't knock it till you've tried it. Sure, the outgoing, self-assured Lion likes to hear herself roar, and naysayers insist that she can be deeply egocentric. But Leo is also sincerely generous, a trait that Taurus both respects and enjoys. Bulls love treats, and have a soft spot for the good things in life, and Leo gets a thrill out of giving. What will the Lion ask for in return? Complete adoration and complete commitment. That's fine with Taurus, who doesn't need to be Mr. Universe (at least, not in public), and who also expects one hundred ten percent from his lover when it comes to loyalty. Leo, take care not to tire Taurus out; stay tapped in to that natural magnanimity of yours, and you'll have your Bull by the horns. Taurus, stroke your Lion's fur and soak up her lavish material and emotional gifts, and she'll be an absolute pussycat.

♍ ♉ **Virgo with Taurus** When Virgo and Taurus get together, there's both good news and bad news. The good news is, when two earth signs unite, they practically spontaneously combust with lust. Between the sheets, life will be grand, even effortless. Virgos tend to have a reputation for being cold fish. In truth, they enjoy sex unabashedly, passionately, and frequently. That suits Taurus to a T. Let's just hope that it makes up for Virgo's out-of-bed personality: they get their kick organizing, planning, polishing, and Making Things Happen. Taurus does not want to be Made To Happen. Taurus wants to be left to her own devices. And she certainly does not relish being criticized—even constructively (unless it's done tactfully, and with something yummy to make it more palatable). Capable, impatient Virgo, tattoo these three words onto the palm of your hand: Choose your battles. Taurus, understand that Virgo is just trying to help. Really. Keep in mind that unless this relationship is carefully finessed, things could get ugly.

♎ ♉ **Libra with Taurus** Wherever Libra is, romance follows. So does perfectionism. Taureans rarely make careless errors, a trait Librans will applaud wholeheartedly. Libra will love his Bull's thorough approach to everything, from lovemaking to concocting the perfect seven-course dinner to balancing the checkbook. Librans love to go the whole hog too, especially when it comes to falling in love. That means they'll be more than happy to indulge the Bull's hedonistic hankering for things that soothe and stimulate the senses. Taurus will thrive under the sunshine of Libra's attention, and that little part of the Bull's psyche that's terrified of being two-timed will almost melt away. Almost. What's the catch? Yes, the Scales are perfectionists. So if Taurus isn't perfect—and who is?—there's a good chance Libra will soon be back on the road seeking the impossible dream. And Taurus will be devastated. This combo is more "short fling" than "the real thing."

♏ ♉ **Scorpio with Taurus** If there's anyone who can handle the sting of a Scorpio, it's Taurus. Possessive and intense (and that's an understatement), Scorpio's attention can seem loving, sincere, and flattering at first—and it is all of those things. But after a while, the sheer intensity of it, continuing unabated, can feel stifling. However, it takes a lot to rattle a Taurus, so possibly a good deal of Scorp's jealousy will roll off her back. Maybe the Bull can focus on the Scorpion's peerless sexual drive and talent. Then again, maybe she can't. Bulls do need time alone. Scorpio, be mindful that just because she's not handcuffed to you doesn't mean she doesn't care—she just needs to breathe, that's all. Taurus, reassure Scorp as much as possible, in both your words and your actions. And Taurus, if you decide you want out of the relationship, gather up the nerve, tear yourself from your comfy couch, and run. There's no other exit.

♐ ♉ **Sagittarius with Taurus** "I have been faithful to thee . . . in my fashion." Taurus, do you buy this line of Sadge's (which she ripped off from the decadent nineteenth-century poet Ernest Dowson, by the way)? You might, with good reason. After all, she means it. Sagittarius is rarely dishonest—just honestly inconstant. And this will piss off Taurus, guaranteed. At first, he'll be charmed by her adorable, outgoing, witty personality; wowed by her many friends; envious of her energy. But monogamous Taurus will not be comfortable with the fact that Sadge has had loads of partners before him—and that she may want to continue to have loads of partners while *with* him. If that's the case, Taurus, bid Sadge a hasty adieu. However, if you get your hands on a mellower Sadge, the pairing could have the makings of a classic opposites-attract love story. Sadge will have you out dancing at least two nights a week—and loving it. And, you'll get your Archer to actually sit down at least two nights a week. Give this relationship a serious go only if you share the same views on monogamy.

♑ ♉ **Capricorn with Taurus** Goats and Bulls. Both have horns, and both like to eat tin cans. Astrologically, this match isn't too far from the Scorp/Taurus pairing, except there's slightly less room for possessiveness and jealousy to enter, since the Scorpion isn't involved. Devoted and sensual lovers, this duo will be tender and gentle with one another both in bed and out of it—most of the time. Bull droppings will hit the fan when Capricorn fears he's not being accepted for who he is. Unlike a Libran, however, he won't head for the hills. He'll hold on with the painful tenacity—and, possibly, manipulative techniques—of a Cancer. This can be avoided by frequent, tangible displays of affection by both Goat and Bull. If it's just a bit of no-strings frolicking in the fields either one of you is after, though, skip it, and go find a Gemini.

♒ ♉ **Aquarius with Taurus** Neither the Water Bearer nor the Bull is flighty or flippant. That's a good thing. However, Water Bearers are traditionally thought of as being cold and emotionally distant. Although not necessarily the case, does it really matter, if that's how it feels to the Bull? Unconventional and very socially conscious, Aquarians are going to be out of the house quite a bit, campaigning for their favorite causes. "Cool," thinks Taurus. "I've got the place to myself." But when the Bull hasn't seen her partner in, oh, a week (except on the 10 P.M. news in a rally), she might start stamping her hooves a bit. Meanwhile, Aquarius views Taurus's mild hedonism as self-centeredness. Can the Water Bearer compromise his social agenda? Can Taurus adopt a more Spartan attitude to life and love? Unfortunately, the answer to both is, *hell, no*. Not a lot of long-term potential here.

♓♉ **Pisces with Taurus** Ah, Pisces: the cosmic-yet-catastrophic Soul Mate. In Chapter 12 you'll find out why the Fish is everyone's soul mate; for now, try to suspend your disbelief. Selfless, sexual, mysterious, and artistic, a Piscean might seem to be everything a Bull could want. And perhaps he is, as long as Taurus's immobility isn't mistaken for being emotionally closed (something Pisces can't comprehend), and as long as Pisces doesn't mess with the Bull's head. In this case, the Fish and the Bull will happily give each other the "me space" both need. The Fish will be allowed to do what he loves best—give—while Taurus has the luxury of sitting back and receiving, and the opportunity to nurture her Fish however and whenever she wants.

3 *the dynamic duo*

GEMINI—THE TWINS, May 22–June 21

Ⅱ   GEMINI'S INTERNET DATING PROFILE

Q: Favorite movie
A: *Catch Me if You Can*

THE REAL ANSWER: *Four Weddings and a Funeral.* (Note: the four weddings are Gemini's. It's your funeral.)

Q: Favorite color
A: Blue

THE REAL ANSWER: A rainbow! Why should I have to pick one color?

Q: Favorite book
A: The latest book on the *New York Times* bestseller list.

THE REAL ANSWER: The review of the latest book on the *Times* bestseller list.

Q: Favorite classic song
A: "Makin' Whoopie"

THE REAL ANSWER: "Always True to You, in My Fashion"

Q: Favorite drink
A: Anything, as long as it's portable.

THE REAL ANSWER: Anything, as long as it's caffeinated and portable.

Q: What is your ideal home?
A: A funky place in an offbeat part of town. There should be lots of room for my friends and significant other, because I like to give parties when I'm home.

THE REAL ANSWER: Who cares? I'm never there. And don't homes come with things called "mortgages?"

Q: Where will you be in five years?
A: My five-year plan is to continue my education. By the end of that time, I will be finishing my dissertation.

THE REAL ANSWER: I already have a master's, so why should I torture myself? In five years, the party will just be getting started.

P.S. Gemini's posted photo will be blurry. The Twins move too fast to be caught digitally.

Getting to Know Gemini

The Twins are so much fun, which is why they've had more dates than you've had hot breakfasts. Join in. Here's your chance to skim the surface, surf the waves, enjoy superficiality. It's so restful after all the angst you experienced in your last relationship. In fact, Geminis are the perfect transition lovers. They don't expect too much from you. They flit in and amuse you when you're bored, then flit out when you want to be alone. Doesn't this sound like the perfect scenario? It is, if you don't think about where they are and what (or whom) they're doing while they're away from your side.

What's in This Relationship for You

Geminis are hard to pin down, but once you do you'll have double the pleasure.

Constant novelty

Obviously, there's much to be said for a Gemini lover. Much will also be said *by* your Gemini lover. If you're into the strong, silent type, go elsewhere. A lighthearted charmer by nature, Gemini is a midsummer night's dream; you will never be bored. So many ideas swirl around inside that cranium that your Twin will seldom be at a loss for ways to entertainment you. Gemini will take you ice skating, and then for a long walk, an expedition to the town square to window shop for antiques, a tour of church flea markets, a detour to a travel agent's to get brochures, and finally to breakfast. Yes, all this and more—even before you've had your morning coffee.

Two for the price of one

What's Gemini's secret—amphetamines? Not really. The reason being with the Twins is double the fun is because Geminis have twice the usual number of personalities. That's why they can out-skate, out-walk, and out-shop you. Try to keep up with them, if you're so inclined. Or just let them go wherever it is they go when you want to be alone. Soon, you probably won't even care what they're doing.

How to Attract Gemini

You may notice that you didn't have to go in search of Gemini. Gemini found you, because he's always in circulation. That's a welcome reprieve for you, after the time you spent hunting down a Lion or tromping around searching for a Taurus. One thing you must do is hold the Twins' interest. If not, they'll forget your name and e-mail address, and even your very existence. Yet, how can you date, much less manipulate, someone who isn't there? For now, try these tips:

Act carefree

Be as lighthearted as the Twins themselves are. While doing mundane tasks with Gemini, demonstrate your gift for skipping through life. At the grocery store, sing along with the songs playing over the PA system. Do you want to have a somber and serious discussion? Don't try it. At this stage, Gem's rule is *personal drama non grata*.

 LESSON Act playful, and Gemini will consider keeping you on the playmate list.

Avoid depth

Geminis dislike depth and won't stick around if you delve. It's stuffy down there, and the journey takes too long.

 LESSON Keep things superficial at this point, or you will be out of the mating game.

Things have happened so quickly with Gemini, your head is spinning. You must get your bearings. You're having a lot of fun, yet, not being an astrological amateur, you've heard about the Gemini split personality. Even if outwardly amusing, this relationship might be inwardly hollow. If it's to last, there has to be some kind of heart connection. So, is there?

How can you find out more about the Twins and what they're like in love relationships? Put out the word among your acquaintances and news will come rolling in. "Lucky you," says one source. "I heard your Gemini wines and dines better than a Leo, and that's saying something. Enjoy yourself!" Another friend phones in, "You're dating that Gemini? Since you really want the truth, the word is your Gemini gets around. That's why he swooped in on you so fast. It's the Twins' style. With all that flitting around, he's bound to catch something—oops, I mean someone. Be careful."

These are obviously conflicting reports. Or are they? No, they're both accurate assessments. Welcome to love and life with a Gemini. This experience truly can be like dating two different people who inhabit one body. What should you do now? Why not act your sign, and ask Gemini direct questions? Start with something unthreatening, like work.

YOU (TO GEMINI OVER DINNER) "I'd love to hear more about your career."

GEMINI "As you know, I'm in communications."

YOU "That sounds fascinating. What a perfect fit for you." (You're thinking about a tech job, or one in media.) "You must have to work with all types of people. Do you write, or are you in advertising?"

GEMINI (PEERING AT THE MENU CLOSELY) "The filet mignon with black peppercorn sauce sounds good. What will you have, my darling?"

YOU (FOR ONCE, NOT BEING THROWN OFF COURSE BY GEMINI'S CONSIDERABLE TALENT TO DISTRACT) "Yes, it does sound delicious. You were telling me about your job, though."

After navigating further attempts by your dinner partner to distract you with charm, you finally discover Gemini holds the position of greeter at a large store. No problem, but it's not exactly the career picture Gemini painted at first.

 LESSON Be firm if you want to know the whole story. It's surprising how willing someone who is actually two people in one likes to deal in half-truths.

The Gemini Deal Breaker: Being Smothered

Gemini is an air sign, and needs to be able to breathe. Make sure to be able to give the Twins space or you won't be sharing a room, much less a bed.

The Committed Relationship: You Got What You Wanted; Here's How to Keep It

You've passed Gemini's test. Gemini, in turn, has passed yours, but you're still going to keep your eyes—and options—open. Now that you're in a relationship, you'll have to adapt to both personalities as they pop up, since you'll be around them for longer than the occasional romp. You'll also get the chance to do a little relationship management (the Gemini euphemism for "manipulating at home"): As an overall strategy, pretend to be superficially as much like Gemini as possible.

Act youthful

Gemini loves youth. Reflective of this preference is Gemini's perpetual curiosity, which he's compelled to satisfy. What's the newest energy efficient car? Who's the number-one box office star this month? Gemini knows. So should you. Their up-to-date knowledge of many factoids helps Twins of even retirement age seem young.

 LESSON Read the news headlines every day. Your erudition will impress Gemini. Meanwhile, you can concoct crafty ways to handle the Twins when problems arise.

Cultivate myriad interests

You're a well-rounded person with many hobbies. You enjoy equestrian sports and running in charity marathons, and can actually sit through a Wagner opera without falling asleep. Add a few more interests, and Gemini will happily come along for the ride.

LESSON The Twins thrive on variety. A Gemini with a set routine is an unhappy camper. And you have to deal with the displeasure.

Throw parties

Are things getting a bit stale? They must be, because Gemini's two personalities pop in and out several times a day. What to do? Invite company over. Gemini is a sociable sign, and works a room even faster than a Leo. Having a variety of guests to talk animatedly to keeps Gemini happy and gives your ear a rest.

Throw parties in the bedroom

These parties are for just the three of you. Having observed firsthand that for the Twins, variety is the spice of life, you proudly acknowledge being the mate of a veritable spice rack. More excited by ideas, Gemini isn't the most physically passionate sign. Somehow, the Twins have speculated that you're boring in bed simply because you said black leather doesn't look good on you. You're about to surprise your lover by revealing many different personalities, all in one evening. First, act dominant by ordering Gemini to strip or face the consequences. Later, transform into a naughty-yet-nice type. Then whisper sweet-yet-smutty nothings in Gem's ear. For the next round, leave the room, then return fully dressed and inquire innocently, "You sent for me?"

LESSON If you play many roles, your sexual virtuosity will dazzle not only Gemini's body, but more importantly, his or her mind. It's the Twins' primary sex organ.

Do's and Don'ts in the Gemini Mating Game

Because this relationship brings up feelings that run the gamut from A to Z, it's easy to forget that "do's" and "don'ts" apply. Here they are:

Do encourage Gemini to see friends often. It's the best way to satisfy that craving for variety, and will help prevent Gemini's eyes—and hands—from roaming.

Do give Gemini space. Partake in activities on your own, and don't under any circumstances make a habit of spending every night at his place. Gemini isn't particularly possessive, but if you circulate it will keep him on his toes.

Do argue. This is really just a conversation starter when the nonverbal Twin makes what promises to be a prolonged visit.

Don't reprogram Gemini's stereo, TV, or DVD remote. The Twins must be informed immediately at all times. If you screw up basic tenets of communication, you probably won't get screwed the way you'd like to.

Don't forget to gossip. News, especially that of his friends and business associates, is the breath of life to Gemini. If you're not the gossipy sort, make up some stories and leave out the names to protect the innocent, also known as the "nonexistent."

Don't call Gemini on small fibs. Save your ammo for the big ones. As delightful as your lover can be, sometimes when the Twins enter a room, the truth flies out the window.

You Want Out: Ways to Leave Your Loser

You've wearied of playing silly bed and head games. Variety has lost its novelty and creative truth is losing its charm. Besides, the multiple facets of Gemini are something a qualified doctor should deal with, not you. It's time your partner moved on. Gem heartily agrees: This relationship has been going on for three whole months and the atmosphere is too stifling. The Twins would rather talk than "have talks." It doesn't take very much to get rid of a Gemini lover. It's harder to keep one. But if using them makes you feel good, here are a few phrases you can toss at your lover on the way out.

- "Do you know how I can tell you're full of it? Because you're still breathing."
- "Do you remember that magazine article you read called "Gold Strike?" You said a huge gold mine was found. Well, it was really about gold miners on strike. Read more than the headlines for a change."
- "You're so proud of your communication skills, but you don't know a split infinitive from a tautology."

Now, *that* one hurt.

Bliss or Bloodshed: How Your Sign Fits with Gemini

♈♊ *Aries with Gemini* See Chapter 1, Gemini with Aries.

♉♊ *Taurus with Gemini* See Chapter 2, Gemini with Taurus.

♊♊ *Gemini with Gemini* Four personalities in one house can make for quite a lot of fun and even more confusion. Let's hope one of you has some sturdy Taurus or practical Capricorn in your chart, or this relationship may evaporate before either of you knows what happened. As with any same-sign match, you'll be comfortable with each other. Because Gem is a flexible sign, you won't have to deal with competitiveness, unlike a dominant Aries who has hooked up with another Aries. Your pairing may be a passing fling or a lifetime match. However long it lasts, take advantage of being with someone who likes to go places and do things. You'll have a good time and retain fond memories of each other.

♋♊ *Cancer with Gemini* Imagine maternal Cancer matched to flighty Gemini. This could be soothing or grounding for Gem. Cancer, you will see your lover adoring all the attention, which brings out the childlike side of Gem's personality. For both your sakes, let's hope this side isn't the *enfant terrible*. Cancer doesn't want to play mommy to an unruly set of Twins. It conjures up visions of diapers, strollers, and two infant car seats taking up space in the back of the car. Gemini, if Cancer tells you, "My Explorer's in the shop," it means you've worn out your welcome. Not even you can talk your way back.

♌♊ **Leo with Gemini** What absolute bliss, thinks Leo, when conjoined with a Twin. Gemini is remarkably perceptive, noticing all of your good points and constantly telling you how fabulous you are all the time. This must indeed be the love of your life. Then you hear the Twins say the same things to other people. It's not fair, but that's beside the point. The point is, does she really feel with the depth you'd expect of your lover—or is it all talk? It depends on the Gemini. Leo, watch your partner's actions rather than listen to what spills forth from her mouth and you'll get a truer picture. And Gemini, are you tired of having to reassure Leo of your love? Find some comfort in all you have in common: certainly not homebodies, you're both into fun, games, and going out on the town.

♍♊ **Virgo with Gemini** Both the Twins and the Virgin are communicators. It's said that knowing how to communicate with a lover is the bedrock of a good relationship. This truth is conditional upon your getting past the talking and moving on to other things, like romance and sex. Another plus exists in this pairing—both of you love to gather information. But there's a difference in method, motive, and execution. You Virgins keep up with current events but are more likely to be focused on one thing at a time. Geminis can be found watching a cable news channel, reading the newspaper, a magazine, and listening to talk radio simultaneously. Is it any wonder you're hip to all the hot topics, Gem? On closer examination, although familiar with the headlines, you don't want to be bothered with all the boring details, such as what was finally decided at the City Council meeting. By contrast, Virgo does want to know. What's the use in knowing there was bond issue debate when you don't know what was discussed? Gemini, put that brilliant mind of yours to work. Jump past the headlines and watch the entire newscast or read the whole article. You'll impress Virgo and learn vital information, as well. If the two of you can engage in talks of substance, this relationship has a good chance of making it in both the living room *and* the bedroom.

♎Ⅱ **Libra with Gemini** This is another natural match. Libra and Gemini are both air signs, which means they're occupied with primarily intellectual matters. Each of you has an admirable detachment that prevents the kind of embarrassing quarrels you see between two super-angry Leos. You're both assets to parties and go out as much as possible. It's great fun to imagine what you'll do together once you get home. Libra, you're more likely to sit back and wait to be approached by friends and admirers, so you won't see much of the intrepid Twins, who couldn't "sit back" at a party if you paid them. Gemini, try not to work the party with the desperate enthusiasm of an actor between jobs. It's so embarrassing to the Scales. Libra, you can see both sides of any issue and appreciate having a lover who is willing to act as a sounding board. Gem, although you're ready to listen, you're probably not much help in pinning down a particular point. Learn to listen and you and Libra can build a great relationship.

♏Ⅱ **Scorpio with Gemini** This pairing could be called *Stranger in a Strange Land* if Heinlein hadn't snatched the title for his classic book. Scorpio, you're a stranger in Gemini's strange land. Reciprocally, Gemini, you're a stranger in Scorpio's strange land. That's why you two can't wait to get together. Scorpio is drawn to mystery and strangeness, and the Twins love to explore the new territory found in Scorpio. With distinctive differences in personality, both of you will learn much from each other. Passionate Scorpios vitalize Gemini's sexual experiences. In turn, Gems are more sociable than Scorpios. The problem that may crop up is Gemini's tendency to keep an eye out for something better to come along. Scorp, you're deep and we realize by now how stifling Gemini finds depth. So concentrate on the good sex, and enjoy this encounter while it lasts. Who knows how long that will be? Even an astrologer is a stranger in this truly strange land.

♐♊ **Sagittarius with Gemini** Though Gemini and Sagittarius are on opposite sides of the zodiac, both signs are freewheeling types who dislike being pinned down (except during activities involving a mattress). Each of you takes gambles. But there's an important difference: Sadge is blunt and forthright, saying, whether tactfully or not, what's on his or her mind. Gemini prefers to be gentler when expressing opinions. To translate this into Sadge language: Gemini is full of euphemisms and at times even b.s. and this bugs the Archer. Gemini, try to say exactly what you mean without first coating it in marzipan to make it more palatable. Your partner likes to hear your words straight and will suspect you're up to something even if you aren't. Sadge, soften your bluntness occasionally. Honesty is the best policy, but it's not always the most effective technique for getting what you want from the Twins. If both of you focus on your respect for each other's freedom, you'll be happier.

♑♊ **Capricorn with Gemini** Conservative Capricorn with gregarious Gemini? Stranger things have happened—every once in a while. Capricorn, you who are so well grounded and practical may be inclined to take on Gemini as a project. Be forewarned: Gemini won't stand for that. Instead, wanting to tempt you into tossing off your conservatism, not to mention your cash, the Twins may lure you to a racetrack. Gem, Cappy does have fun—it's just not your idea of amusement. Both of you probably see each other as a reform challenge. Capricorn, as a trade-off let Gemini take you rollerblading and in return, persuade him to reconcile his bank statement. If you're both willing to compromise, you'll be more open to betting on this match's romantic potential.

♒♊ **Aquarius with Gemini** As both Aquarius and Gemini are air signs, this is a good match. Both love personal freedom and give it to each other freely. Aquarians have more staying power than Gemini. They're also more eccentric, but Gemini doesn't really care about that. However, what Aquarius perceives as Gemini's lack of caring can cause problems. The Water Bearer tends to care a great deal about one (often political) cause or another. Gem, you may embrace one of Aquarius's interests enthusiastically, but lack the Aquarian ability or inclination to follow through. Though the Twins make splendid politicians, if not for their campaign advisers, they'd forget where they were due to deliver their next speech. So, Aquarius, let

Gemini help when he or she is able. In return, Gemini not only will tolerate what other folks call your weird ways, but will even brag about them to anyone who'll listen. And with you two wild ones, what is life like in your bedroom? Let's *so* not go there. This isn't that kind of book.

♓ ♊ **Pisces with Gemini** Elusive Pisces and getaway driver Gemini: will they pair up? Probably. Both signs like to try new things. Pisces, you can sympathize with Gemini's need for freedom. You share this need, though you don't talk about it. You just give, and give, and give until you can't stand it any more, and then disappear—temporarily. Pisces, take note: If you stage a disappearing act, even a Gemini will panic. If Gemini wants some alone time, he or she will tell you. Try communicating with the Twins—who continually change emotional frequencies and whose attention span is too short to tune into you empathically—by using words rather than nonverbal cues. And Gemini, awaken your intuition (or borrow someone else's) so Pisces will feel connected to you. This match could take some work, but don't let that deter you. Even matches made in Heaven need to be nurtured.

4 *the cosseting crustacean*

CANCER—THE CRAB, June 22–July 23

♋ CANCER'S INTERNET DATING PROFILE

Q: Favorite movie
A: *One Fine Day*. George Clooney and Michelle Pfeiffer fall in love in the midst of trying to watch each other's kids, and save their own jobs. So cute! To say nothing of the cameo made by New York dessert-spot Serendipity Café's luscious frozen hot chocolate and ice cream sundaes. Yum!

THE REAL ANSWER: *Tropic of Cancer*. Moody American dude trolls around Paris in search of money, food, and sex—my three favorite things. (Not that *I'm* ever moody.)

Q: Favorite song
A: "Unchained Melody." Romantic, and reminds me of that sexy scene in *Ghost*.

THE REAL ANSWER: "I've Got You Under My Skin." And that's where you're going to stay, whether you like it or not.

Q: Favorite drink
A: Milk. Good for the kids, good for me!

THE REAL ANSWER: Hot chocolate with a dash (or three) of brandy and crème de menthe.

Q: What is your ideal home?
A: New England country chic, definitely. My kitchen will have loads of old-fashioned pots and pans and ropes of garlic hanging from the ceiling. In the living room, all the furniture will be made out of hewn pine, and the bedroom's pièce de résistance is going to be a patchwork quilt. [Note: Cancer, you have been refining this dream for an entire lifetime. God help you if all you have is a cold-water flat in a sixth-floor walkup.]

THE REAL ANSWER: Whatever and wherever it might be, it's *mine*, dammit! And don't even *think* about trying to help with the decorating.

Q: Where will you be in five years?
A: Vice President of Operations in a major New York publishing house.

THE REAL ANSWER: Stay-at-home dad.

Getting to Know Cancer

You really needed to get out, because you just ended a fling with a headstrong Aries with a bang, not a whimper (sadly, par for the course with Aries). You've ended up at a holiday party thrown by a friend-of-a-friend. You were never really into the holidays, truth be told, what with all the tinsel and bright, shiny lights and "cheer." Anyway, floating around looking a little lost, clutching your flute of sparkling wine like a security blanket, you end up at the hors d'oeuvres table. Suddenly, when you look up from a platter of crab dumplings, you see a darkly handsome, capable-looking gentleman with a smile on his face and a fresh tray of those very morsels you'd been sinking your claws into. You smile back, and Mr. Crab Dumpling offers to refill your glass. When he does, he pops a fresh cranberry into the bubbles, and presents it to you with a flourish. Hey! Suddenly you *are* feeling festive, after all. What sort of magic is this?

This is your host, and your host is a Cancer.

This little choose-your-own adventure tale could turn out a few different ways. Most likely, though, you and Cancer eventually sink into a sofa in a dimly lit corner of the room, sharing deep thoughts until Cancer smells something burning, and realizes that he left the mini-pizzas in the oven all this time. After he rescues them, he runs back to you, deeply apologetic and with a full bottle of champagne. At the end of the night, you feel bubbly yourself, a bit tipsy, and very much like a Natural Woman. What's more, Cancer wants to cook you dinner tomorrow night—dinner *à deux*, he's quick to point out.

"Merry Christmas! Happy holidays! Happy birthday!" you tell yourself, giving yourself a little squeeze. "I found a Cancer in my holiday stocking." Go ahead and rejoice—with caution.

Possibly the most nurturing sign in the zodiac, your Cancer will love to take care of you. Rest assured you'll never want for a home-cooked meal, a willing ear to be bent, a pair of hands to help you set the house to rights after *your* holiday party, and your very own interior decorator.

In other words: You've got Mom. And that can be a great thing. Ruled by the moon, Cancers are super nurturers, talented in and enthusiastic for all things domestic, and, like Virgos, they love to help. Be prepared to come home and find your dry cleaning hanging neatly in your closet, the mail—sorted, slit open, and stamped with the date of receipt—waiting for you on the counter, and a freshly vacuumed living-room carpet. Yes, Crabs treasure domestic bliss above all else—usually if *they* control it. They crave being needed both physically and emotionally, and being homebodies doesn't mean they're not highly capable leaders, a trait that is especially handy in a pinch. Perhaps you come home from work one evening to find your cell phone bill has arrived. You tear it open, expecting something around the usual $39.95, but blanch with fear when you see $1,505.42. What?! You know you went over your limit a bit, but this is ridiculous. While you collapse, pale and shaking, at the kitchen table with a gin and tonic, Cancer will rally to your cause, call the cell phone company, and have everything straightened out before you add another lime slice to your drink. "No problem," says your Crab, sweetly. "They just forgot about your free-nights-and-weekends deal, that's all. Your new total amount due is $54.17."

Whew. Thanks, Mom.

However, there's a downside to a mother's love. It's very easy for Cancer to step over the line into excessive loving, once she's gotten her claws into you. Okay, you say. If that happens, I can just nudge her back over to the less stifling side of the line, can't I? Well, only if you're *über*-diplomatic, because once Crabs feel rebuffed—even if the slight was unintentional—they'll retreat into their shell, and then turn around and scuttle off in search of another sign. Or, if it's a more serious or long-term relationship, they can turn cold, manipulative, and vindictive. This can make your life miserable. Beware.

What's in This Relationship for You

There's no love like a mother's love. You'll find that out fast when you start seeing a Cancer. Prepare to be petted, pampered—and pinched—within an inch of your life. Okay, so that sounds a little scary, but take heart. In the words of a famous melody, "It Ain't Necessarily So." Crabs do, in fact, have more than one virtue to recommend them; here are a few.

Nurturing

It's the dominant Cancerian trait, so if you're in need of a little TLC, you've come to the right place. Maybe an Aquarius has just ditched you in favor of a long-term attachment to the World Wildlife

Federation (check out Chapter 12 to learn more about the Water Bearer's fondness for good causes). Remember coming home from college for winter vacation after a round of nasty exams, and how Mother let you sleep until noon for a week and nursed you back to health when you came down with the inevitable end-of-the-stressful-semester flu? This is the kind of physical and spiritual coddling you can expect from a Crab. You'll forget all about that airheaded Aquarius as your Cancer bathes you in a warm glow of affection and comfort.

Loyalty

When Crabs are in a relationship, they're committed to it, pure and simple—and they'll expect the same from you. Stay on your Cancer's good side, and you'll never have to worry about her cheating heart. Period.

Stick-to-itiveness

Like Taurus, Cancer is doggedly, often maddeningly, tenacious. Those pincers may look small, but boy, are they tough. This means that the Crab is willing to weather the ups and downs of a relationship. By corollary, they also like to hold onto what is theirs. Ownership, and lots of it, makes them feel safe. You won't catch Cancer blowing her whole paycheck on a wild night out with the girls, but she may well invest it all on a brand-new KitchenAid mixer (or three). If you need to borrow something, Cancer probably has it, and will be happy to lend it generously to you. KitchenAids, Band-Aids, lemonade; just ask, Partner of Cancer, and ye shall receive.

How to Attract Cancer

How do you get your claws into a Crab—or better yet, get her claws into you? You could try to seduce maternal Cancer by donning a diaper, sticking a pacifier in your mouth, and whimpering, "Mama," if you're into that kind of thing, that is. Most likely, however, you won't have to go to such lengths: the Crab in question will respond well to traits that mirror her own. The impression you're trying to convey is, "I'm at the top of my game, personally and professionally; I have taste, class, and, most importantly, cash; and, ultimately, I know what I want, Cancer, and that's you." Here are a few tips to make it easier to grab a Crab.

Look gently seductive

Gentle, nurturing Cancer wants to be enticed, not taken by storm. Leave your all-black Goth gear in the back of the closet, and wear warm colors on a first date. This doesn't mean you have to look like the Easter bunny; just focus on shades like dark or pale orange, brick reds, and rich browns. Complement your outfit with tasteful jewelry. Ladies, save your four-inch stilettos, plunging necklines, and leather pants for a date with a Scorpio. For a casual coffee with Cancer, don a chocolate-brown, funkily floral shirt over a pair of perfectly fitted jeans, paired with yellow slides. The look is cute and comfortable, and says, "I am a relaxed, emotionally available individual." Guys, skip the biker jackets and ripped dungarees, and stick with well-groomed basics, like clean khakis and a pressed blue shirt. Now is a good time to wear those silver cufflinks that are collecting dust in your top drawer. A Cancer chick will be attracted by classy simplicity.

Be grounded

Don't act like a flighty Aphrodite. Cancer is in his element with folks who are down-to-earth, sensitive, and trustworthy. So even if you're not, pretend you are, and Cancer will let down his guard. If you're at a party with a Cancer you want to snag, don't be overly flirtatious. Sure, work the room and chat with whomever you like, but avoid any obvious hair tossing, giggling, and exchanging of starry-eyed gazes with other men. And whatever you do, don't get drunk. Cancer will not be interested in a wild child. Focus on the Crab in question when you're with him, and when you leave him, say a slow goodbye with sincerity, intensity, and even a kiss on the cheek. He'll be bewildered and visibly hurt if you leave him in the dust while you sashay off to the bar with your best guy friends.

Pay for things

Cancers aren't cheap, but they view your financial security as their financial security. In other words, the fact that *you* have it means *hers* won't be threatened. It's unlikely that a Cancer woman will take offense when a suitor picks up the dinner check, opens the door for her, rises from the table when she does, or performs any other traditional honor-thy-woman gestures. Quite the opposite: Not only is Cancer impressed by fiscal stability, she tends to be a bit of a traditionalist when it comes to etiquette. On a first date, gentlemen, bring your credit card with you. As you're waiting for your table, go to the bar and bring her a drink. Treat her to a luscious meal, and don't even let the check arrive at the table; ask the maître d' to hold it at the bar or reception desk. Don't worry; next time, your lady will offer to pay, and you should let her. First, though, show her that you're an old-fashioned charmer, in the best possible way.

The Cancer Deal Breaker: Rejection, Either Real or Perceived

Take note of the word "perceived." You don't have to flip Cancer the bird to wound him. It can happen very easily by accident, especially if you're a more thick-skinned sign, like Sagittarius. When a Crab *thinks* he's been slighted, he will act as if he *has* been slighted. What's the difference, your Crab will point out, between *thinking* I've been hurt and actually having *been* hurt, if I *feel* hurt?

Logically, of course, there's a big difference; but the consequences for you as Cancer's lover will be very similar. Cancer is a water sign, and effects of rejection, either real or imaginary, will ripple within his depths for miles.

Say your Crab's spent the afternoon in the kitchen, concocting one of his majestic apple pies. (Cancers love dessert in all its forms, by the way.) He's excited because:

1. The kitchen smells great
2. The painstaking latticework crust came out perfectly
3. He gets to feed you, one of his favorite hobbies

But you went to lunch with your chocoholic sister earlier that day, and splurged on flourless chocolate torte with spumoni on the side, followed by an Irish cream on the rocks. Sweets are the last thing on your mind. But if you refuse at least one slice of Cancer's crowning glory—his apple pie—expect serious sulking until at least the following morning.

On a larger scale, perhaps you head out for a few after-hours drinks with coworkers. You don't bother to call home since you don't expect to be long, but when you finally glance at your cell phone, it's 10 P.M. and you already have three rather snarky text messages from the Crab. Crap! You hightail yourself home, and find Cancer waiting for you on the couch.

"Was Eddie from accounts there?" he asks. He's suspected you for months of having a crush on said Ed, even though that's the farthest thing from your imagination. Answering honestly, you make the mistake of confirming that Ed was present. You've cooked your own goose, honey. Now you're in for Crabby petulance for at least a week, and all this sulking just might be more than you can take.

The Committed Relationship: You Got What You Wanted; Here's How to Keep It

The best way to nip Cancer jealousy in the bud and to keep insecurities at a minimum is profuse verbal and physical reassurance. Sure, everyone needs to be reminded of their partner's commitment, but Cancer needs such reminders 24/7. Tell him you love him . . . and that you want to rip his clothes off in public. Let him know with a growl how hot he looks in that new suit. Purr that you love the way he takes care of you. Then walk the walk: Make a point of holding hands in public (the Crab loves it when the world can see that you belong to him!); initiate sex as often as possible, and during it, be very, very vocal; when he's washing the dishes, sneak up behind him, wrap your arms around him, and smother him with kisses.

 LESSON Frequent physical contact reminds Cancer that he's the one you want—and it makes *your* life a whole lot less painful.

Pretend Cancer is your mother. I've already enumerated the ways in which Cancer acts similarly. Now, if you wanted to keep Mom happy, what would you do? Mind your manners, for a start. Remember that the conservative Crab tends to be very traditional, at least where etiquette is concerned. So open the car door for her, and offer her your hand while she's getting out. If she drops something, be a gentleman and pick it up. And for goodness sake, mind your table manners. Sloppy soup slurping and loud chewing will be a huge turnoff to Cancer.

 LESSON Treating Cancer like a prince or princess is guaranteed to keep the Crab happy. She's a big believer in that do-unto-others adage; show her that you care for her as much as her nurturing personality shows you she cares for you. Minding your proverbial P's and Q's around her is one way to do just that.

Keep your own claws in your trousers. This goes for both sexes (whether you're wearing trousers, a skirt, a bikini, or a Speedo). Again, the Crab can conjure up plenty of reasons on his own to be insecure. Chances are there's little to no truth to them, but that doesn't matter if Cancer believes there might be. So don't give him any reason to think there could be any substance to those nightmares he's been having involving you, your boss, and a pair of crotchless panties (on *both* you and your boss). This is true for most relationships regardless of star sign, but even more so with Cancer: if you feel like cheating, something is wrong with your relationship and it needs to either change or end. If you grow bored with your Crustacean and seek out a mollusk or two for a bit of extracurricular beachside fun, you're only making life harder for yourself. Cancer, whose intuition is legendary, will find out. And when he does, it won't be pretty.

 LESSON Illicit affairs might seem like fun, but the repercussions of Cancer catching you outweigh the benefits. A flightier, more sexually liberated sign might react differently, but the Crab is just too vulnerable. If you feel like spreading your wealth around, you might first want to rethink continuing the partnership.

Do's and Don'ts in the Cancer Mating Game

Do learn to apologize. (Yes, that goes for you too, Aries.) It's not that Cancer is self-righteous or won't admit when she's wrong. It's just her old insecurity rearing its ugly head again. If the Crab feels you've hurt her, say you're sorry even if it wasn't really your fault.

Do give Cancer control over his home environment as much as possible. Some signs don't care where they sleep, as long as it's warm and dry. (Sadge doesn't even care much about that.) A Cancer's house is truly an extension of himself. Of course, if he's sharing that home with you he'll have to compromise—just let him feel that his home is his own.

Do accept the Crab's displays of tender, maternal love. Rebuking them is as good as rebuking the very essence of Cancer himself.

Do ask her to do things for you. This neat little trick ensures that Cancer will coddle you in ways you actually *want* to be coddled.

Don't let your moods get the best of you. Sensitive Cancer, often very moody herself, will take others' moods very personally. Try especially to avoid outbursts of negative emotions, since it'll rattle Cancer for days afterward.

Don't be judgmental. No one likes being judged; Cancer won't stand for it.

Don't insist on dragging Cancer away from home for too long. Understand that Cancer needs to connect with her home to connect with herself. If you do keep her away for ages, don't be surprised when she becomes antsy and crabby.

Don't ignore Cancer when he tries to talk about his feelings, even if he approaches you awkwardly. Crabs care for others easily, but don't often talk about their own emotions or needs. If he's telling you how he feels, listen attentively; it's important.

You Want Out: Ways to Leave Your Loser

You're fed up. You knew Cancers had trouble with trust, but this is ridiculous. Your Crab has been in a mood for weeks, convinced beyond a doubt that you're seeing someone behind his back—even though you've been absolutely faithful. And this isn't the first time his insecurity has morphed into jealousy and run amok. At this point, you've had it; you want to be sympathetic to Cancer's fears and sensitivities, but they're running—and ruining—your life. Plus, Cancer's too serious, already thinking about Pampers, mortgages, and private school—and you've been seeing each other for only six months! How can you pry your Crustacean's claws from the hem of your robe?

It won't be easy. You could plead, cajole, say you're just not ready for that kind of commitment, yada yada yada. Talking will get you nowhere. Nor, surprisingly, will refusing to eat the elaborate meals Cancer cooks for you. Cancer will just hold on tighter. If you've considered cheating, now might be a good time to do it. If doing so takes too much time and effort, or your pesky morals hold you back, you just might have to tell the Crab, "It's all true. I never loved you in the first place." Whether it's true or not, Cancer's ingrained insecurity will buy it—and trade you in for a new child . . . um . . . lover.

Bliss or Bloodshed: How Your Sign Fits with Cancer

♈ ♋ *Aries with Cancer* See Chapter 1, Cancer with Aries.

♉ ♋ *Taurus with Cancer* See Chapter 2, Cancer with Taurus.

♊♋ **Gemini with Cancer** See Chapter 3, Cancer with Gemini.

♋♋ **Cancer with Cancer** It's an even 50/50 here; there's the potential for long-term loving, but it's also possible that you two might kill each other with kindness (or unkindness). Two Crabs will be more than willing to nurture each other and be loyal to the end, but since Cancers can be very moody and reluctant to discuss their emotions, even with a significant other, lack of communication could come between you. Still want to make a go of it? Try to remember that you're not solely responsible for each other's moods—and that a little alone time is like Brussels sprouts: you may not like them, but they're good for you.

♌♋ **Leo with Cancer** Can we say "codependent," boys and girls? Learn how, because this match inspired the term. Not that that's necessarily a bad thing. Leo, you prima donna, if you're not adored, cherished, fawned over, and mollycoddled at all times, you flip. Cancer, you desperately need someone to mollycoddle. Perfect? Possibly. Just keep your expectations reasonable: Cancer, understand that your Lion will have other admirers; Leo, your Crab will want you to stay in a few nights a week. Can you make a deal? Try. It might be worth it.

♍♋ **Virgo with Cancer** Two of the most helpful signs in the zodiac, the Crab and the Virgin are very similar.; They love to plan, can come across as just a little bit controlling (pardon the understatement), and thrive like hothouse flowers on security. Also, both are serious homebodies. Sometimes too much of a good thing is a bad thing, but not in this case. The biggest problem you two will run into is, who's going to be in charge of remodeling the kitchen? Then again, that might indeed be quite a challenge. Seriously, though, the Cancer/Virgo hookup has the potential to become a loving, functional, and trusting—if intense—relationship.

♎ ♋ *Libra with Cancer* Romantic Libra will charm Cancer at first. The Crab loves doting on her partner, and it's so nice to be doted upon in return. "Finally," the Crab thinks, "I've found someone who knows how much difference the little things make." Libra slips a note into his Crab's lunch box, or surprises her after work, whisking her off to a hot new restaurant. Cancer is in Heaven! You might run into trouble, though, if Libra's social life explodes. Remember to let the Scales breathe—and that Libra is super scrupulous. Two little words that might save the relationship, Cancer? *Don't worry.*

♏ ♋ *Scorpio with Cancer* If anyone can match a Scorpio's jealousy, it's Cancer, even though the Crab's jealousy stems from a different source, insecurity, as opposed to the Scorpion's egotistical possessiveness. Until they try to cohabitate, Cancers and Scorpios are going to get on reasonably well, unless they give each other reason for doubt (very unlikely), or unless Cancer withholds sex. When Crabs and Scorpions move in with one another, however, heads and claws will fly unless they each have their own, very distinct responsibilities and domains. Scorp, do the weekly shopping—alone. Let Cancer do the cooking, without input from you. The result: domestic bliss.

↗ ♋ **Sagittarius with Cancer** There's no way to sugarcoat this: A Cancer with a Sagittarius is like the lighting in a department store dressing room—blindingly painful. It's not that a Crab and an Archer can't love each other. It's just that they will annoy each other mightily. Sadge can't stand being smothered; unfortunately, smothering is what Cancer does best. Sadge is a traveler; Cancer, a homing pigeon. When the Archer stays out till the wee hours with friends of the opposite sex, the Crab will be unreasonably suspicious and Sadge will feel unreasonably frustrated. Plus, the combination of these issues makes it very, very hard to talk to, much less trust, each other. Neither of you needs to suffer this much. Skip it.

♑ ♋ **Capricorn with Cancer** Dogged determination characterizes both these signs. Determination by the two of you to be together is a good start. Additionally, both Goats and Crabs thrive on emotional, financial, and physical stability. Cancer respects Capricorn's responsible nature and love of elegance and quality. (With Sadge, you get weekly telephone calls from Brussels or Zimbabwe; with the Goat, you receive diamonds, MP3 players, and gifts from Saks Fifth Avenue.) Cap soaks up Cancer's subtle sexiness and daily doses of affection. The only snafus are that you're both stunningly predictable and take ages to reveal true emotions. But when you do share from the heart, it'll be for keeps.

♒ ♋ **Aquarius with Cancer** Cancer and Aquarius both love fiercely. Cancer loves Aquarius fiercely; Aquarius loves the whole world fiercely. Once in a while, Crabs will, in fact, renege on their ultraconservative lifestyles, and head out in search of something different. In other words, they'll engage in flings. When you get that yen, Cancer, grab the tail end of a passing Aquarius, and learn a thing or two about being passionate, impulsive, and sexually inventive. Aquarius, take Cancer by the claw, and carve out time from campaigning. Relax on Cancer's couch, and let the Crab make you bacon-wrapped scallops and a great martini. Then, while things are still sweet, for God's sake get out.

♓♋ *Pisces with Cancer* Instant soul mates? Just add water, *à la* sea monkeys? Pisces will open her fins and embrace the Crab without reservation. Cancer's snagged, hook, line, and sinker. The Fish thinks his Crab is a little reserved emotionally, but is confident he'll "crack that shell." Meanwhile, the budding romance is intriguingly mysterious. And boy, do both love to love. A strong bond could develop, as long as Pisces curbs his tendency to bend the truth and Cancer takes care not to overwhelm. The Crab can't stand a liar, and the Fish needs to be able to swim freely. If you can both let down your defenses long enough, the two of you sea monkeys just might be able to make it work.

5 *the enthroned beloved*

LEO—THE LION, July 24–August 23

♌ LEO'S INTERNET DATING PROFILE

Q: Favorite movie
A: *The King and I*

THE REAL ANSWER: *The King and I.* It's so nice to see a film about myself and whoever plays "I."

Q: Favorite color
A: Gold

THE REAL ANSWER: Gold. And it's not a color, it's a state of mind.

Q: Favorite Classic Song
A: "It Had to Be You"

THE REAL ANSWER: "Unforgettable." That's what I am.

Q: Favorite book
A: *Burke's Peerage*

THE REAL ANSWER: Anything written by Lord Byron, a warrior *and* a romantic. What more could anyone ask?

Q: What is your ideal home?
A: A nice comfortable house suitable for entertaining. I like to host parties. There'll be a wet bar and swimming pool, not to mention a hot tub. Drop by anytime.

THE REAL ANSWER: A "comfortable" home—are you kidding? I want a castle with all the trimmings. People can stop by anytime they want to, as long as I'm not tied up with the prime minister.

P.S. The posted photo will be of the real Leo—but airbrushed and highlighted.

Meet His Royal Highness

Think back to your high school days for a moment. Let's say you're a girl of sixteen, your hormones are raging, and you can't stand your biology teacher.

You're standing by your locker, and with a gasp, you see That Guy walking down the hall toward you. Well, he's not really walking; it's more of a strut, swagger, and hip wiggle all rolled into one hairspray-melting package. He is, of course, the most popular boy in school. You're madly in love with him—and so are all your girlfriends. He occupies most of your gossip time at slumber parties and in intricately folded notes you pass back and forth to each other in study hall. Once, after you had drunk half a wine cooler your mother had inadvertently left on the counter, you confessed to your best friend that you'd already picked out names for the three children you'd have with him (Taylor, William, and Miranda).

Don't be embarrassed by that memory. Sure, it was a teenage, giggly, girly crush—but you weren't crazy. Everyone loved That Guy, and no one could help it. His magnetism and smile were just too hard to resist. Chances are, That Guy was a Leo.

Imagine how it would have felt if he had strolled up to you, slid a muscular arm around you, and said, "Hey, babe. You and me. Friday night. How about it?"

You'd swoon, hundreds of envious cheerleaders would glare at you viciously, and all the football players would eye you with newfound respect. You'd be on top of the world.

That's exactly what dating a Leo is like. If you've snagged one, prepare your heart for the kind of leaps and bounds it hasn't enjoyed—or suffered from—since your sweet sixteenth party. Dazzling, flamboyant, charismatic, and irresistible, Leo just may be the most fun sign in the entire zodiac to date. And the best part is, most of the time the Lion's charm isn't staged for effect. No, the Lion sincerely cares about her adoring fans.

(Write "adoring" on your hand in pink ballpoint ink; tattoo it on your left arm inside a heart. To a Leo, it's the most important word in the world.)

So what's the downside to dating a Lion? Can there be a bad side, with the good time that's being had by all? Most definitely, yes. Along with all that charm comes a great deal of pride, which can swell up into a full-blown attack of arrogance and egocentricity, often when Leo suspects that he's not being adored as much as he should be. Suppose you and your Leo lover go to that new, hot Brazilian bar next to your office for a coworker's bon voyage shindig. The Lion hasn't met your colleagues yet, many of whom have become good friends over the years. Both of you enter the bar, and a cheer goes up from the crowd of your caipirinha-chugging chums. Leo puffs out his chest proudly—until he realizes the cheer isn't for him, it's for you. You're instantly inundated with handshakes and hugs, and the guest of honor presses a lime-laden glass into your hand. Watch Leo—he's sulking. His winning smile has disappeared. Then, after a few minutes, the Lion's chest reinflates, as it hits him: This is *his* hot-stuff date everyone fancies. Suddenly, all is right with the world again.

Moral of the story? Even when pride goeth before his fall, Leo usually can't resist his own inimitable charm.

What's in This Relationship for You

Like enthusiastic, outgoing Sadge, Leo loves people openly and sincerely. This means that the Lion's a blast to be around, even when the attention's focused on her—which it will always be.

A generous spirit

Leos are fun, fabulous, and only occasionally fake. There are many benefits to being the monarch's consort. Uninformed people say Leos can be self-absorbed, tyrannical, and touchy, but this is nothing more than a misconception. The Lion's good points are well known. He or she is generous, compassionate, and open to flattery. If these traits sound too boring, then just think of all the ways you can twist them to your advantage. One warning: Leos are strong, so if you think flattery is the only weapon you need in your arsenal, think again.

Hot sex

Leo—the good kind, that is—is one of the best romantic bets for a long-term, sustained sexual connection. Lions are loyal, in spite of the constant presence of that group of admirers you will come to refer to as the Leo Entourage. A happily committed Leo will rarely fool around. But if you continually cease to show interest in meeting his or her needs, well, the Lion is only human.

How to Attract Leo

Leo people were born under a sign that is both proud and generous. So the Lion is generous enough to show off others besides himself and will be attracted to a trophy mate to display as well. Before you rush off to find a mirror to see how your reflection holds up, stop and consider. Yes, Leo is one of the signs to whom appearance is important.

 LESSON Make sure you look your personal best whenever in Leo's presence.

Good looks aren't the only thing the Lion looks for. A Leo academic will grade you by the number of diplomas you have; an athlete won't wrestle with his conscience when he counts how many laps you can run at the track; and a Leonine art fan may give you the brush-off if you can't name at least three members of the Fauvist movement. A trophy of some kind is required of a lover, who must be able to be one as well. Luckily for you, each Leo defines "trophy" in a different way. Unluckily for you, you're still being judged. It's a nerve-racking but necessary ordeal if you want to consort with the Lion on an intimate basis.

Now you have a taste of the early stage of the relationship. So, you've met lovely Leo and want to make an impression. It seems a challenge, given that she is surrounded by pesky admirers. But don't lose heart—you can make yourself stand out. Try these tactics.

Notice Leo

Let's imagine you and Leo are at the same social function. Look at the Lion often. It means you're friendly and outgoing, as is she. It also indicates you have good taste. Leo has a heart of gold, and it's well worth winning even if you aren't mercenary.

Set yourself apart

Because Leo is such a lordly sign, people pay homage to it. That seemed fun to Leo at first, but it's like eating dessert all the time. Everyone bows and scrapes, taking obsequiousness to a new low. Stand out by being cheeky. For example, now that you're within conversation range of the lofty Lion, try something like the following.

YOU (APPARENTLY ADMIRING THE LEO APPEARANCE) "Did you choose that shirt yourself?"

LEO "Why, yes. Well, at least the salesperson picked it out for me."

YOU "By the look of that fabric, he must've had a bone to pick with you."

 LESSON Draw Leo's attention to you by being spunky.

You've really attracted Leo's attention now. Mutual friends—a married couple—saw both of you chatting and witnessed the sparks flying. The well-meaning couple knows you'll get along well. Besides, you look good together and would make great dining room decorations at future dinner parties. So they play a matchmaking game—and bang, you've got a drinks date next Thursday. To ensure you capture Leo's interest and, later, his heart, try the following.

Compliment Leo

Leo is a vessel waiting to be filled with compliments. Some people will trot out all-purpose flattery by saying, "I love your shoes," or "Nice car." However, you won't make the cut if you fall back on the "impersonal obsequiousness" routine. Notice that the above compliments are given to what Leo *owns*, not what he *is*. Compliment the Lion on his accomplishments.

For example, offer something like this, "Cassandra tells me you've just been appointed department head at the university. That's quite an accomplishment, especially for someone so young." You've become someone who sees the specifics of the Leo persona—the real Leo—and the Lion appreciates that. In his eyes, your comment was perceptive, flattering, and reassuring. Yes, Leo exudes confidence, but his or her ego actually needs strokes and reassurance. If you compliment only Leo's Lexus, how will the car's owner know if you'll stick around after it's traded in for the next model? Leo wants to know it's the Lion you're lusting after, not the Lion's accoutrements.

 LESSON Personalize your compliments. And stick to sincerity.

Let Leo do the talking

Given the opportunity to tell his or her story, you can bet the family gold futures that Leo will. Begin with a conversational gambit like, "Cassandra tells me you're not from this area, and that you've had an interesting history. What's your journey been like?"

Leo looks ecstatic, and begins to tell the story. "It all started when I was a youngster. . . ." Just listen, and Leo will give you a turn to talk about your life—eventually.

What's the key to this successful technique? When chatting up Leo, you used the word "your," and two variations of the word "you." The personal interest in your conversational partner demonstrates to Leo you have sound priorities. Furthermore, your queries about the Lion's life opened up a subject Leo finds endlessly fascinating.

 LESSON Unlike secretive Cancer and mysterious Pisces, who enjoy staying silent because they're private people (and doesn't that just bug the heck out of you?), Leo revels in revelation.

Yes, the Lion loves a good listener. You've proven you can be a potential royal subject. Prepare to enter Leo's kingdom.

The Leo Deal Breaker: Disrespect

As we've seen, Lions have a lot of pride. Serious insults about Leo's career progress or family show discourtesy. You're being even more disrespectful if you humiliate the Lion in public. Does this mean you must tiptoe around Leo all the time? No, just watch yourself in public. If necessary, you two can duke it out in private.

The Committed Relationship: You Got What You Wanted; Here's How to Keep It

The previous suggestions worked, and now you're a couple. Before you take the final royal oath of allegiance, though, be alert to signs of possible incompatibility. Let's say this particular Leo, a male, is a part-time art lover, as are you; but you're the kind of girl who's also interested in music and movies. Leo has already tested you on your academic accomplishments, athleticism, or art knowledge. You tried on the glass slipper and it fit. Now present Leo with a glass loafer: Give him a compatibility test.

For example, suggest going to a revival of the film *Amadeus*.

YOU (WHISPERING THROUGH MOZART'S SERENADE FOR WINDS, THIRD MOVEMENT) "This guy was amazing. He composed a symphony and wrote his first opera by the time he was thirteen."

LEO (AFTER HE FINISHES SWALLOWING A MILK DUD OUT OF GOOD MANNERS AND DEFERENCE TO YOU) "Yeah, but what was his batting average?"

You stifle a giggle and dart a glance in his direction to make sure you both don't succumb to uncontrollable laughing fits: a phenomenon that often happens in places in which you're supposed to be silent. Then you notice that Leo has resumed his consumption of Milk Duds and shows no outward signs of amusement.

 LESSON If Leo's not laughing when you are, watch out. In the long term, a cultural compatibility problem might cut short both your laughs.

Let Leo Persuade You to Do Something You Don't Want to Do

Leo has pride, and needs to be proud of you, as well. Maybe you're on your guard after the Mozart/Milk Dud incident. Or perhaps you're after a Lioness who gave you a withering look when she discovered your diploma lacks the word "*magna*" before "*cum laude*." In any event, the bottom line is that you're miffed on a night that Leo wants your attendance at a very important event: a cocktail party being thrown by Leo's boss.

YOU "I'm tired. Besides, I don't want to go."

LEO "Why? Are you angry with me or something?"

YOU "No. I'm furious. You didn't have to call me a cretin in front of the docent at the art museum just because Picasso was the only Fauve I could name. I do know what the word fauve means. It means 'wild beast' and now I can name another one."

LEO (IMPRESSED BY YOUR KNOWLEDGE OF FOREIGN-DERIVED WORDS AND YOUR EAGERNESS TO INCREASE YOUR ARTISTIC IQ) "That's exactly what it means. Another Fauve is—"

YOU (INTERRUPTING WITH GREAT RELISH) "You!"

Leo is temporarily speechless. Although on the verge of taking umbrage at your insult, he's also considering what will happen if he shows up at the party without you on his arm. Having decided that coaxing you into quaffing corporate cocktails is more important than Fauvism, artistic or personal, Leo seeks to soothe you.

LEO "You look so great in that dress. Everyone will be envious of me and jealous of you."

YOU "Envy. Is that all you think of? I'm not a trophy. Am I made of silver? Do I have big handles attached to my head?"

Before you continue your tirade, stop and think. You can have a fun evening out, basking in the compliments you invariably get when wearing that dress. So put away your unbecoming angst and slip into your best cashmere coat. At the party, work the room with all the poise and professionalism of a member of a royal family at a diplomatic event. Also, stick to Leo and act fascinated all night even if you have to fake it.

Why bother? After all, you won't get the satisfaction of watching the big cat suffer for his heinous crimes—Leo's pride prevents out-and-out groveling. But be patient. If a Leo is wooing or loves you, your forbearance is soon to be rewarded. The next night, Leo surprises you with a gift. It might be a Waterman fountain pen or gold jewelry. If you prefer a different metal to adorn your desk, pocket, or person, wait until later in the relationship when Leo has done something really wrong. That's the time to seize on the subject of platinum.

 LESSON If you acquiesce to Leo and give a command performance, you'll be richly rewarded.

Do's and Don'ts in the Leo Mating Game

Do remember the Lion likes compliments. Give them often. Underneath every Lion is a pussycat who constantly needs to be stroked.

Do act jealous. You don't actually have to be. Some signs shrink from jealousy, and conjure up visions of extreme cases that can slide into stalking. But Leo finds it flattering rather than felonious; it means he or she's important to you.

Don't be disrespectful. This point is worth stressing, because you'll become too stressed out to remember how to manipulate Leo if you push her on this deal breaker. Lions can be magnanimous to a fault, but one thing they can't stand is attitude directed toward them.

Don't make Leo feel left out. Your partner likes for you to be around all the time, even if you're not interacting directly. What if you're in desperate need of alone time? To get Leo off your back without hurting his feelings, tell him someone else wants to see him. Leo knows you just talked to a mutual friend (let's call her Sarah) about another pal who's at loose ends this evening.

> **YOU** I haven't seen Jimmy in a while.
>
> **LEO** I haven't either.
>
> **YOU** Sarah said he was asking about you.
>
> **LEO (PERKING UP)** Really?
>
> **YOU** I think he's a bit proud and doesn't want to make the first move. Why don't you call him and see if he wants to do something tonight? The State Fair is going on right now.

Leo bounds to the phone and makes arrangements to meet Jimmy at the midway. Expect him to come home sticky from cotton candy and carrying a well-deserved teddy bear won at the ring toss.

 LESSON Coming to a friend's rescue makes Leo feel wanted without causing him to feel unwanted by you. Send him on this errand of mercy and you'll get your alone time.

Don't forget to spice up your sex life. Leo love is a constant. To other signs, like Aquarius or Pisces, that could be boring or exhausting. Any relationship needs the occasional sexual jump-start, and yours with Leo is no exception. One good way to do this is to cry wolf. When he is out running a routine errand, call him. Pretend something's wrong. Say the sink's backed up or the puppy is stuck in a tree. Once Leo comes to the rescue, wave your plunger in the air and show off your clear drains. "I guess you busted me," you confess coyly. Then seduce Leo. Leo smiles at your confession as it dawns on him that it was him you wanted, not an odd-job man. Even though the Lion knows he's been had, he'll have you, with pleasure, in return.

You Want Out: Ways to Leave Your Loser

Okay: you thought you'd nabbed a noble, generous, and selfless Leo. You hate to admit it: you were wrong. Perhaps "duped" would be a more accurate term, because Leo successfully concealed his or her tyrannical side. Don't kick yourself. Monarchs are trained from birth to display pomp regardless of the circumstances. You were so blinded by Leo's kingly charisma that you failed to read all the royal decrees. Or, you noticed all the signs, but the fun of manipulating faded into "managing" things tactfully. How exhausting.

Maybe Leo is feeling a little raw, too. The Lion wants more respect, time, and attention than you can deliver. It's time to call it quits. You can do the job nicely, leaving bridges unburned and your dignity intact. Or you can get malicious satisfaction by adhering to the following template.

- Insult Leo's taste in everything (except mates, of course).
- Treat Leo like a child. When on the golf course together, snatch off the Lion's cap and put sunscreen on the royal face, chiding him within earshot of fellow golfers, "You always forget to protect your complexion. You'd be lost without me." Now Leo will consider you no big loss and you're free to leave.
- Be indifferent. It's the unkindest cut of all.
- Stop having sex.
- Compliment Leo's best friend constantly, remarking on how successful and good looking the friend is. Eventually, your soon-to-be ex will pass you over to the pal (that is, if you aren't there already).
- Harp on Leo's inadequacy in the most vulnerable area: Say you faked orgasms (or used erection-enhancing substances without prior disclosure).

Need to play any dirtier than these suggestions allow? Again, though, don't underrate the value of an intact bridge. Leave with dignity, and just vent to your best friend. Later, you'll be glad you did.

Bliss or Bloodshed: How Your Sign Fits with Leo

♈♌ *Aries with Leo* See Chapter 1, Leo with Aries.

♉♌ *Taurus with Leo* See Chapter 2, Leo with Taurus.

♊♌ **_Gemini with Leo_** See Chapter 3, Leo with Gemini.

♋♌ **_Cancer with Leo_** See Chapter 4, Leo with Cancer.

♌♌ **_Leo with Leo_** When one Leo is presented to another, they'll both bow and smile and try to figure out who has the most power. You'll feel a natural sexual chemistry, and be curious as to whether or not this will follow you into the bedroom. It will. But competitiveness can be a problem. Constantly one-upping each other could turn your game of spin the bottle into a contest over who can dump the other the fastest. Both of you need a companion you can respect. Yet neither of you truly wants someone whose strength threatens yours. The success or failure of this combination depends on whether or not one of the partners will bow before the other. There can be only one absolute monarch in this relationship and it takes a rare Leo to take on the role of continual consort. Flexibility is the key here. In any dispute, Lions can roar all they want. But if you want the relationship to last (instead of this coupling to be your last), put pride aside or all you'll have is a short but heat-filled encounter to show for it.

♍♌ **_Virgo with Leo_** There are few things Leo relishes more than sparkle, and few endeavors that industrious Virgo likes to do more than make things sparkle. Leos adore assets and Virgo is an asset to any relationship. This may not be the stereotypical "we fell in love across a crowded room" match, but it can succeed because Virgos will work hard to make it a go. And also because Leos are loyal: once a commitment is made, Lions will demonstrate admirable ability to stick to people and to their word. The real question is: will there be enough chemistry to pull the two of you together in the first place? If so, Virgos must realize that all work and no play make Leo a dull mate—or an ex-mate. Continue to court your Lion. Tap into your creativity to pen love notes, or plan a romantic vacation. Leo, the way to reach Virgo is to emphasize your organizational ability. This, rather than extravagance, earns big points with the Virgin. Suggestion: Set up separate checking accounts so Virgo won't experience the pain of watching large sums of cash flow out of it.

♎ ♌ **Libra with Leo** Libra's smooth social skills are an enticement to Leo. Libra certainly knows how to give a classy party. Both of you are upwardly mobile without being snooty about it. The two of you, likely to be attracted to each other, will also be good friends. This pairing isn't as much of a snore as it seems to be. Leo, you're comfortable enough with Libra to talk about what's happening in your life, and to take advice, without losing face. Libra, if you're going back and forth with your decision-making scales, Leo can stop the dizzying motion and offer a firm suggestion. We've covered compatibility. What about romance? Leo and Libra are two of the most outwardly romantic signs of the zodiac. The only contest here will be over who can come up with the most romantically imaginative treats. Yes, this match is sweet.

♏ ♌ **Scorpio with Leo** Scorpio is drawn to Leo's light, and Leo to Scorpio's mysteriousness. You two will discover the joy of opposites attracting, and you'll find each other strangely fascinating because of your significant differences. There is common ground, though: Both of you are passionate. Sparks will fly at first. Then, farther down the road, you may be dueling with sparklers if you can't smooth out your incongruities. Nevertheless, the relationship can work because Scorpio is happy to be the power behind the throne. Leos like to be *on* thrones. Leo, remind Scorp how to have fun, and teach him or her to lighten up (without using that exact wording, of course). There are pluses to this pairing: you're both in it for the long term—neither of you gives up easily. The primary problem you face is one of control. Leo may be the monarch, but if it becomes too apparent that Scorpio is the *éminence grise,* Leo will put the proverbial foot down. Even if things sometimes go sour, both of you can be too stubborn to give up and will gladly serve a life sentence without parole. Don't give each other a hard time, or you'll end up doing hard time together.

♐ ♌ **Sagittarius with Leo** Think of a Beach Boys song. Its sunny lyrics and up-tempo melody will give you a good idea of what this match is like. Both of you like to have fun, and this is another powerful sexual chemistry match. Sadges don't give a damn about who's in charge, and will gladly let the Lion take the reins—that is, until Leo tries to rein you in. Leo, give Sadge room to roam. Your playmate will return happier and more appreciative of your company. And Sagittarius, we all know how well meaning you are, but sometimes a blunt comment will seem like a sharp pinprick to Leo, deflating the ego and hurting pride. Watch these sensitive areas, and together you can spend time on life's beach having fun, fun . . . well, you get the idea.

♑ ♌ **Capricorn with Leo** Let's call this one "The Monarch Meets the Chairman of the Board." You'll understand each other's need for success, although conservative Capricorn may cringe at the seemingly smarmy sales style Leo employs. Leo, you probably want Capricorn to loosen the tie and have fun. Why don't you two meet in the middle? Have fun and do business at the same time. Is there a colleague of Cap's in the West Palm Beach office? Use that as an excuse to get away and take in some sun; Capricorn's "must-be-productive" urges will be satisfied, too.

A possibly troublesome spot is romance. Capricorn may possess deep feelings, but Leo needs to see them to believe them. Yet Capricorn dislikes public displays of affection. Here's a tip: compromise. Capricorn, display your affection in tangible ways. Hold Leo's hand. That's not too tacky, is it? Leo, remember the Goat doesn't wear his or her heart on the sleeve. If Capricorn doesn't kiss and caress you around others, don't take it too personally.

♒ ♌ **Aquarius with Leo** This pairing can be like a Republican with a Democrat or Robespierre with Louis XIV. Unless Aquarius is willing to interact more personally with Leo and devote more attention to him or her than to "the group" that usually occupies Aquarian time, the Lion will feel neglected or ignored. Aquarius, invite Leo to be your date at a fundraiser for your pet cause. And Leo, loosen the leash you try to lead Aquarius around with. Better yet, get rid of it completely, if you're able. Aquarians are rebels and buck authority of any kind, a tendency that may have the potential to clash with Leo's monarch persona. Make an effort to respect each other's differences and nurture the love in your relationship. Do you both want flowers and champagne? Respect and pay attention to your mate on a personal level, or you'll be on the receiving end of a posy of nettles and a Molotov cocktail instead.

♓♌ **Pisces with Leo** Goodness knows Pisceans love to please the one they love, which is music to Leo's heart. On the surface, an outsider might think it's easy to attach a glib label to this relationship: Leo is dominant and Pisces is submissive. It's not that simple (nothing is, when the Fish is involved). Pisces is blessed with gifts of elusiveness and passive aggression, and will sneak away while Leo is busily bossing. Leo likes self and possessions to be on display and thrives around people. Pisces prefers secrecy. What to do? Pisces, lavish attention on Leo. Doing so comes naturally to you. Leo, be generous with your praise and show appreciation for the nice things Pisces does for you. And if things get really sticky, indulge Pisces's secrecy fetish. On a date, engage in some role-playing. Pretend you're both committed to other people, and are sneaking around behind their backs. Yes, this game may seem extremely silly, and it is. But it turns the Fish on, so why not give it a try?

6 *the velcro virgin*

VIRGO—THE VIRGIN, August 24–September 23

♍ VIRGO'S INTERNET DATING PROFILE

Q: Favorite movie
A: *Help!* I just adore helping. I can do everything from sewing on buttons to untangling fishing lines.

THE REAL ANSWER: *Looking for Mr. Goodbar*

Q: Favorite color
A: White. It's so pure.

THE REAL ANSWER: White, the color of most of my household washables. It's so easy to maintain. From sheets to shirts, all I have to do is use bleach. I also love to wear white because it reinforces the myth that Virgos are virginal. It helps if I'm propositioned by some undesirable, because I can act naive. And if someone suitable and sexy approaches, I can look unsullied, like a virgin, and act like a . . . well, feel free to finish that sentence as you like.

Q: Favorite book
A: *Oxford Book of Quotations,* the Quiller-Couch edition.

THE REAL ANSWER: *The Kama Sutra*

Q: Favorite classic song

A: "Brush up Your Shakespeare." Cole Porter was a genius as a songwriter, and an excellent role model for all who aspire to elegance. He was also a millionaire who worked even though he didn't have to.

THE REAL ANSWER: "I Fall to Pieces." I'm being ironic—I never fall to pieces. My day planner would never allow that.

Q: Favorite drink

A: Bloody Mary

THE REAL ANSWER: Virgin Mary. (Another little joke.) I like martinis, hold the vermouth, ice, olives, and swizzle stick.

Q: What is your ideal home?

A: A warm, cozy home with clean, simple lines on the outside and no tacky chintz inside.

THE REAL ANSWER: A house that's easy to maintain. It would be nice to have ground cover instead of a lawn to save on lawn-mowing fees.

Q: Where will you be in five years?

A: Taking my first vacation.

THE REAL ANSWER: Living in the same house, working for the same company, and earning a much larger salary . . . *and* taking my first vacation.

P.S. Virgo's photo will be perfect.

Getting to Know Virgo

Virgos are usually pigeonholed as nitpicky neatniks with little romantic feeling and no interest in sex. Read on to get a realistic glimpse into a relationship with a Virgin.

It's a lovely autumn day: the leaves are just turning golden, and the temperature is still comfortable enough for you to wear summer clothes. Exotic victuals are spread on a blanket before you. Between nibbles, you offer your companion a few entertainment choices.

YOU "We can chat or lie here and enjoy the day, or I can read a poem to you."

VIRGO "Oh, poetry, please."

YOU (PICKING UP YOUR COPY OF *QUOTING KEATS FOR QUICKIES*) "I met a lady in the meads/I set her on my racing steed—"

VIRGO "May I interrupt? The phrase is 'my *pacing* steed.' Also, you left out a couple of lines."

Now you're flushed, and it's not with passion.

VIRGO "By the way, it's a ballad. Otherwise, you're doing a lovely job. Keep reading."

YOU "No thanks. Let's do something else."

VIRGO "Yes, let's. Just over that hill is a mountain-bike trail with a secluded spot nearby. Let's make love there."

This sexy voice—and the proposition—is coming from the very same source that just corrected you as if you were a school kid. Suddenly, you're flushed again—this time, with lust. You have visions of thrashing about on the ground, getting twigs in your hair and dirt burns on your knees. Pack up the picnic, and mentally add Band-Aids to your shopping list.

Is prim, proper Virgo really suggesting this escapade? It's one aspect of Virgo, at any rate. The above hypothetical encounter gives you an idea of which Virgo stereotypes are true and which aren't. Can the Virgin be critical? Sometimes. Can Virgo be lusty? You bet, with the right partner. But whatever else, he or she is always practical. So don't be surprised if the Virgin had the foresight to pack a clean blanket, several condoms, and a packet of Wet Ones.

What's in This Relationship for You?

Virgos are earthy and sexual. They also possess a quality of purity. Even if your Virgo was once an exotic dancer, she will still retain the sheen of sexual freshness. Some people aren't perceptive enough to pick up on Virgo's earthy side, so they pass him or her up for a more obviously sexual type, like Aries or Scorpio. But those discerning souls who see past the façade will find a lover who not only can have wild sexual encounters, but also knows how to clean up after them. There are additional benefits that come with the Virgo love package.

Devotion

Virgos love to do things for the one they love. (They also love to do things for most anyone who asks, but that's beside the point.) Many help others to such a degree that they slip into sacrificial mode and become martyrs. What's more, they're smart enough to discern what needs to be done before you even ask.

One day you're going through your closet and find a few shirts that are missing buttons. "I really should find time to sew," you think. Soon afterwards, you and Virgo are going out on the town and you can't decide which shirt to wear. You ask Virgo's opinion: first, because you respect his judgment; second, since Virgo will tell you anyway; and third, because you've finally figured out the best way to prevent Virgo from telling you how to run your life is to ask him first.

> **YOU** "What about the white shirt with the blue stripes?"
> **VIRGO** "I like it, but why don't you wear the maroon Egyptian cotton shirt?"
> **YOU** "I would, but it's missing a button, and I don't have time to sew it back on before we leave."
> **VIRGO** "Look again. I noticed some of your shirts needed attention, so I took care of them. I hope you don't mind."

No, you don't mind. Virgo loves to do things for you. Be magnanimous and allow these gestures to take place.

Criticism

Yes, Virgo is devoted. And, also being smart enough to figure out what should be done, many Virgos take these qualities to an extreme and end up being overly critical. The Virgin isn't putting you down—at least, not intentionally. Rather, your lover is trying to be helpful. Lesson: When Virgo makes too many "suggestions," tell him or her to back off. Or just remember how nice it was to have a button sewed onto your favorite shirt, and hold your tongue.

How to Attract Virgo

To attract one, you should know one thing: What's acceptable to Virgo once a relationship has officially begun is different from what's okay during the seduction phase. During the latter, be refined; use tasteful innuendo. After the relationship is underway and Virgo has let his hair and his boxers down, then you can bring on the smut. For specifics, see the following.

Look good and behave impeccably

To attract a Virgo, be sure your clothes look especially tidy and you are scrubbed clean. Virgo prefers someone who is no stranger to water, washcloths, and loofahs. You should also use your "I'm out to get a raise" manners.

 LESSON Virgo gets off on good grooming and good manners.

Express interest in Virgo's career

Because Virgo's a certified workaholic, no seduction would be complete without a career discussion. (Note: You ambitious Capricorns and competitive Arians have a natural advantage here.)

 LESSON Many other signs like to leave work at the office. But with Virgo, talking about work is a shameless seduction technique.

Act like you're open to renovation

Renovation is usually a word associated with buildings. But Virgo relishes improving people and the way things are done. Most folks think they must be perfect to attract a Virgo. One of the biggest surprises has to do with romance and Virgins. They expect a lot from themselves, and are ruthlessly judgmental when it comes to their own shortcomings. But they love spotting flaws in a potential romantic partner—it's a chance to do a life makeover. So, be open to sharing a few minor problems.

 LESSON Let a few flaws show. Virgo's idea of hell is being involved with someone who doesn't need them.

Before you make a commitment, you should get to know your intellectual, earthy, and versatile Virgin. It's the first flush of love, lust, or maybe just infatuation. You have conversations that last hours (you have so much in common). Virgo likes dogs, and so do you. Each of you has a brother. The Virgin even likes music. My God, this must be your soul mate at last. Before you go so far as to mate—or worse, let Virgo worm his way into your soul—find out more about your new crush.

There are several ways to accomplish this. You could hire a private eye, Google him, or even stalk him. Maybe it's better to try the following simple quiz first. Your manipulative skills will be tested, though, because Virgo must never realize this you are conducting a test. We'll use the word "he" in this example, but the technique applies to both genders.

> **YOU** "I've always dreamed of becoming a novelist. Just think, I could be the next Iris Murdoch, Virginia Woolf, or Jackie Collins."

VIRGO "Cool."

YOU "I thought I'd get my feet wet by writing an article first. Would you mind helping me do a little research?"

You used the magic word, "help," and Virgo agrees. Now come up with a list of ten to twenty questions about relationship issues that are most important to you, yet either are too personal or seem too threatening to bring up at this stage of the relationship.

Then one night as you're sitting by the fire, put your hand on Virgo's thigh and say, "I've been thinking about the article and My Book"—always refer to it in capital letters, so he'll think it's the most important goal in your life—that, and washing his socks. "So may I ask you what you think of my literary efforts so far?"

His answer will tell you a lot. He probably won't want to seem like the kind of guy who stomps on your dreams, so chances are, he'll play along. After all, he did promise to help. If he responds, "Gosh, sweetheart, I don't know anything about literary stuff," he either:

- Doesn't want to hear about your hopes and dreams, in which case dump him, or
- He thinks Iris Murdoch is a kind of flower, and truly doesn't know anything about literary stuff. If so, it's a signal that this Virgo is probably sincere.

You'll know the second possibility is true if he adds, "Even though I don't know much about this, go ahead." Now you can ask questions and glean information about his early family life, openness to having children, and number of previous sexual partners.

The Virgo Deal Breaker: Neglect

Do not neglect Virgo, your relationship, your appearance, your house or apartment, or your career responsibilities. If you do, the Virgin will initially try to help, but if you don't shape up, he or she will give up on you.

Do's and Don'ts in the Virgo Mating Game

Do keep your space tidy. Virgo gets the jitters if surrounded by too much clutter.

Do say "thank you" when Virgo helps, even if you were helped to do something you didn't want to do.

Don't make scenes in public. It's okay to scream at home in the bedroom, but if you so much as raise your voice in public, you'll be the unhappy recipient of verbal vitriol—in private, of course.

Don't change anything in your partner's space. Object placement is part of Virgo's set routine. Don't tamper with the toothbrush, move the mop, or screw around with the shower massage settings.

The Committed Relationship: You Got What You Wanted; Here's How to Keep It

Heed the following advice to keep your mate happy.

Respect Virgo's schedule

Virgos always make out schedules. Although flexible about revising it if it doesn't work, the schedule–whether his or yours—retains its importance. If Virgo wants you to do something you'd rather not do, use this sacred document to get your way. "I'd love to go for a Sunday drive with your great-grandfather instead of playing tennis, darling, but it's just not on my schedule."

Keep your own schedule and to-do list

Slap your to-do list on the wall next to your side of the bed. Virgo will be impressed by your organizational abilities. Later, she will also peek at your list to see how to improve it.

Respect Virgo's workaholism

If you have problems being in a relationship with someone who puts in a lot of overtime, engaging in this romance is wasting both your time and Virgo's.

Be responsible about sex

It's your responsibility to put fun between the sheets on your mental schedule, and subtly remind Virgo to put it on his or hers. As noted earlier, Virgos aren't virginal in the physical sense. They very much enjoy sex. But they're likely to look upon it as another task on their to-do list. Be responsible for making sure it stays at the top of the list—or at least before the laundry.

You Want Out: Ways to Leave Your Loser

This task is a hard one, because Virgo's heart is in the right place. Your lover genuinely can't understand why you think all those caring suggestions are criticisms. Even with his or her finely tuned ability to discern, Virgo can't see that the helpful hints come across as stinging sarcasm. Your self-esteem is in shreds, and you've got to leave in order to protect yourself.

Virgo is clueless about a few other issues, as well. What's wrong with working a lot of hours? Why can't you see that putting the remote control on the left side of the table lamp is much better than on the right side? What's the problem with answering the phone during dinner and with telling you to do the dishes as soon as Virgo hangs up? Why do you get angry when Virgo points out a better route to take than the one recommended by AAA?

Tossing criticism back at Virgo won't work, because the Virgin is immune to its effects. You can't even declare, "This isn't working," because Virgo will find a way to make it work even if it leaves you both miserable in the process. There's really only one way to ditch a devoted Virgo: Say, "I don't need you."

Remember how hard Virgo is on him or herself? And how this trait sometimes slips into martyrdom? You probably feel guilty about leaving the Virgin. Don't kick yourself. And don't kick Virgo—he might enjoy it.

Bliss or Bloodshed: How Your Sign Fits with Virgo

♈ ♍ **Aries with Virgo** See Chapter 1, Virgo with Aries.

♉ ♍ **Taurus with Virgo** See Chapter 2, Virgo with Taurus.

♊ ♍ **Gemini with Virgo** See Chapter 3, Virgo with Gemini.

♋ ♍ **Cancer with Virgo** See Chapter 4, Virgo with Cancer.

♌ ♍ **Leo with Virgo** See Chapter 5, Virgo with Leo.

♍ ♍ **Virgo with Virgo** Help. That's what you'll both do. Since helping other people is the Virgo mission in life, you'll be more than happy to assist each other. You're both good communicators, so neither of you will have any difficulty telling the other exactly how best to run his or her life. That's where the trouble starts. You're both accustomed to being the one with the plan, with the solutions to problems, who never loses socks on laundry day. You could end up in a one-upmanship tussle that makes a fight between two ferocious Rams look like a Junior League flower-arranging competition. Take turns supporting each other. Better yet, as intelligent people, join forces and do some volunteer work for charitable organizations.

♎ ♍ **Libra with Virgo** Libra, you are such a natural at communicating tactfully that Virgo's suggestions sound extremely critical. (Some of them *are* extremely critical.) Virgo, even when you don't mean to sound sharp, your speech can affect Libra like the sound of fingernails scratching a chalkboard. So, follow Libra's lead and soften your observations. Instead of saying, "I'm allergic to that laundry detergent and you know it. I wrote the correct brand on the shopping list," try instead, "I really appreciate your doing the shopping this week. I might have to go again and pick up the dye-free laundry detergent. Would you like anything while I'm there?" Libra will get the message, and probably will volunteer to make the trip.

Libra, you can learn Virgo, too. You're very outwardly romantic, and like to receive little love tokens, voice mail messages saying "I love you," and other common courtship gestures. These tokens of affection may be missing from Virgo's romantic repertoire. If it's important to you, tell Virgo what you want. Also, remember that the way Virgo shows you love is through the kind things he or she does for you. That's worth more than the frequent "I love you" declarations flippantly tossed out by other signs while they're sneaking around behind your back.

♏ ♍ **Scorpio with Virgo** Scorpio, you know what to do; Virgo doesn't need to remind you. In fact, the Virgin's promptings about keeping dental appointments, filling the car with gasoline, and turning off the stove before leaving the house piss you off because they imply that you're incompetent. Relax. Remember, this is how he is programmed. Virgo, you're a communicator and feel uneasy when Scorpio stays quiet. Sometimes silence is the sign of imminent sulking, but usually it means Scorpio wants to be alone and needs privacy. This doesn't mean your relationship is in trouble. Use the free time to do something that gives you pleasure, like reorganizing your closet, and you'll both be happy. Otherwise, you two are compatible sexually. Virgo, you may like Scorp's style in bed so much that you won't insist on changing the sheets before you fall asleep. Now, that's a healthy sex life.

♐ ♍ **Sagittarius with Virgo** An Archer with a Virgin is an interesting pairing. As you'll read in Chapter 9, Sagittarius is willing to give most any relationship a whirl. Virgos are more selective. Jealousy isn't typically a Virgo trait, but the Virgin may weary of seeing a different companion in the video footage from each of your many vacation trips. You might even hear some cutting remarks, like, "Now that was *who*? You've gone on so many trips with so many different people, maybe you should add a cast list to the end of the tape." Jolly Sagittarians will probably laugh. It may take months of similar goading for you to realize that Virgo is not only serious, but also seriously displeased. There's nothing you can do to change the past, but you can stop rubbing your partner's nose in it. Virgo, you'll really have to hold your criticism. To Sagittarius, it brings back nightmarish visions of authority figures giving him or her the third degree. And yes, we know you're practical and Sadges often lack this particular trait. But while you think you're just being real-istic, Sadge thinks her ideas are being shot down rather than sup-ported. Make it clear that you mean to encourage the Archer and help turn her visions into reality. Sadge will brighten up. Then, you can sift through the outlandish ideas and see if some of them can add spice to your sex life. Bet they will.

♑ ♍ **Capricorn with Virgo** Capricorn and Virgo are both earth signs, which means they're practical, steady, and industrious. Sounds sexy, eh? Those qualities *are* sexy to Goats and Virgins. Planning for the future, watching stock market reports, and not spending a single penny unless they have to is this couple's idea of passion. It's a natural pairing that could easily lead to marriage, or at least a permanent shacking-up arrangement. You won't spend *all* your time working late or reading the financial section of *The Times*. You'll also enjoy time together in bed, proving that Aries, Leo, and Scorpio don't hold the franchise on hot sex. Enjoy yourselves, Capricorn and Virgo.

≈ ♍ **Aquarius with Virgo** It's a bit weird to find a Virgo with an Aquarius. That's the very reason you Aquarians will run off and try it. You like being viewed as odd. Virgo feels the opposite way. The Virgin may have a two-sided persona (that of the sexy Virgin), but is, in the end, more traditional than Aquarius. Of course, maybe if the Water Bearer hooks up with one of the radical Virgos who'll eat nothing except organic foods, he or she can revisit the good old hip-pie days. It doesn't matter that Aquarius is too young to remember that free-spirited era, it's the idea that counts. Unfortunately, Virgo counts everything, such as how many times you've gone out with your pals and the increase in household toilet paper consumption since you entered the Virgin's life. If there's anything an Aquarian dislikes, it's being monitored. So, Virgo, lighten up or Aquarius will rebel. And Aquarius, don't rebel just for the sake of rebelling. To make Virgo happy, designate one night as "traditional night." Now, for an Aquarian, that would really be radical.

♓♍ **Pisces with Virgo** Pisces and Virgo are opposites on the zodiacal wheel, yet you have much in common. You both enjoy doing things for other people. Actually, "compulsion" may be a more accurate word than "enjoyment." Your goals are the same, but you go about reaching them in different ways. Pisceans give without judging the recipient. Virgo judges, but helps anyway. Remember to give to each other. As with all opposites, there will be sexual attraction between you two. Can you keep the chemistry alive? A lot depends on how you treat each other. Virgo, as monarch of scheduling, will have to let Pisces follow his or her own schedule. While it's true that Pisces doesn't have an outwardly tangible schedule, there is a personal rhythm she must follow in order to stay happy. Virgo, respect that, and Pisces will respect you. This relationship offers mutual regard as well as good sexual chemistry—what a novel combination. Go for it.

7 *the randy romantic*

LIBRA—THE SCALES, September 24–October 23

 LIBRA'S INTERNET DATING PROFILE

Q: Favorite movie

A: *Sabrina*——definitely the original version. Audrey Hepburn played the part of a romantic and idealistic young lady with panache. Humphrey Bogart triumphed in a role that required balancing the image of a cold, calculating businessman with who he was underneath, a true romantic.

THE REAL ANSWER: *Sabrina*. I can't decide between the original starring Audrey Hepburn and the remake with Julia Ormond. She stepped right into Audrey Hepburn's role, yet made the role her own. On the other hand, though, the original is a classic. It combined . . . (Note to reader: Libra, weighing the relative merits of each version, has run out of space.)

Q: Favorite color

A: A soothing shade such as light purple. Maybe it would be more accurate to say mauve. Violet is nice, too.

THE REAL ANSWER: Mauve——well, mauve and violet.

Q: Favorite book

A: *Persuasion*, Jane Austen's masterwork.

THE REAL ANSWER: *Persuasion.* I also like to skim through Socrates in the original Greek. It's the origin of the Socratic method, a form of logic that comes naturally to me (and law professors, for some reason). I've been told I'd be a good lawyer, though I'm unsure if that's a compliment. Maybe . . . (Note to reader: Libra, trying to explain why her sign confers powers of persuasion possibly hazardous to the health of your relationship's health, has exceeded the word limit.)

Q: Favorite classic song
A: "Isn't It Romantic?"

THE REAL ANSWER: "Isn't It Romantic?"

Q: Favorite drink
A: A glass of champagne, chilled to just the right temperature.The Real Answer: Champagne, silly. As a drink, isn't it romantic?

Q: What is your ideal home?
A: A plush house that's suitable for entertaining. It must have a three-car garage, so there will be room for my two cars, and my partner's.

THE REAL ANSWER: See posted answer.

Q: Where will you be in five years?
A: In a committed relationship.

THE REAL ANSWER: In a committed relationship; not necessarily the next one.

Getting to Know Libra

What's your romantic ideal? Maybe it's a lover who remembers anniversaries and birthdays and is unfailingly considerate—someone who shows commitment by pitching in as a team member. A partner who'll still be romantic and eager to please you ten years from now, not just during the courtship stage. Sounds fair . . . and fairly unlikely, right?

Not necessarily. Let's take another angle into account: fairness. It's underrated as a relationship criterion. Not many people look for love saying, "I want a mate who's fun, adoring, loving—and fair." As many of your friends will remind you, "Life isn't fair, bucko." Dare, despite the naysayers, to voice your wish. There will be dissenting voices, notably Libras, who stand up for fairness and justice for all.

Imagine the statue that represents justice. Wearing a flowing robe and holding a sword in one hand and the scales of justice in the other, she sports another accessory: a blindfold. Libra embodies both images: that of the hopeless romantic and the epitome of justice. What a compelling blend! "I *can* have it all!" you exclaim. "All I have to do is sneak up on and snag a Libra." Looking at it from yet another angle, it's not that simple. Just keep in mind the following: Justice is blind. Love is blind. But Libra isn't.

What's in This Relationship for You

Not much—besides romance, attentiveness, an active social life, and a partner who has the earnest desire to be part of a couple. Remember, Libra is the astrological sign that represents marriage.

Commitment-phobes should stay away. Or should they? To answer this question, ask your Libra prey about his past. For the purposes of the following example, let's say you're dealing with a Libra man, but the example applies to either gender.

Early in the relationship, you observe that Libra's house is beautifully decorated. The dining table is adorned by an arrangement of freshly cut flowers. Throw pillows are artfully arranged on the couch. In the library, shelves are filled with books, ranging from mystery novels to philosophical works by Socrates and a variety of French authors, most of whom are named Jean-Paul something-or-other.

There are also a number of framed photographs. You look more closely, expecting to see photos of little Libra and his family. You spot them—alongside a picture of your man with a woman. Willing to give the benefit of the doubt, you assume she must be a sister. Then you notice that they look intimate enough to have come straight from an early John Irving novel.

YOU "Nice pictures of you and your family."

LIBRA (WITH UNFAILING POLITENESS) "Thank you. I miss them, of course, but not as much now that I've met you."

YOU "And your sister lives where?"

LIBRA "I don't have a sister."

YOU (PICKING UP THE PHOTOGRAPH AND SHOWING IT TO LIBRA AS IF YOU WERE A PROSECUTING ATTORNEY WHIPPING OUT EXHIBIT NUMBER ONE) "Then who is this?"

LIBRA "Oh, her? My second wife. But don't worry, we're divorced."

You certainly hope so. Libra smoothly changes the subject by offering to show you the rest of the house. While you're with him, his smiles and attentiveness reassure you. It's only when you're on the way home that you become annoyed. Why display the picture? Do you really want to become spouse number three? Worse yet, is he really divorced? Calm down and grow up. Libras have pasts, especially the more mature Libras. They're relationship junkies. Some of them even get married as an excuse to throw another bachelor party.

 LESSON Ask Libra directly about his romantic past so you know what type you're dealing with: the keeper or the one-year-stand type.

Don't be diverted by dimpled charm or other tactics devised to steer you off the subject. You need a direct answer so you can decide if this is the man for you. If you give him the thumbs down, hunt down another Libra. And don't worry if the new one is on the rebound. Libras are usually either in love or falling into or out of it.

 LESSON If you're reluctant to date someone who's on the rebound, you'd better bound off and date some other sign.

Take heart, though. Once Libra's finished with a love relationship, it's "out of sight, out of mind." That's why he keeps the photo of spouse number two. Without such a reminder, he'd forget she existed—along with the monthly alimony payments.

How to Attract Libra

Needless to say, Libras are right up there with Leos when it comes to romance. To lure Libra's attention and keep it, start by showing you're up to her standards. For a first date, she will probably choose an old standard like dinner. Why? It's a manners minefield, that's why. Your escort wants to see if you'll use the right spoon when the gazpacho arrives. Or if you'll be gauche enough to exclaim, "Yikes, the cutlery is cold," when presented with a chilled salad fork. Why not just ask you straight out if you're *au courant* with fine dining? Because doing so would be rude.

Try the following tactics to maneuver your way through the etiquette exam. It's a prime opportunity to show off the fact that you know a few things yourself.

Be even-keeled

You're dining at a restaurant where dinner for two costs as much as your monthly car payment. The waiters are taking their time, and you're tiring of making small talk over bread and pâté. It's been nearly an hour, and even the salads haven't arrived yet. How do you get some service? Do you call out, "Hey, waiter! We should call ourselves 'waiters'—we've been sitting here for a long time. Any chance of hurrying up the mixed baby greens topped with balsamic vinaigrette and pine nuts?"

You'll attract their attention, all right. You'll also lose Libra's. Instead, silently catch the eye of a passing waiter, motion him over to the table, and quietly enquire about the status of your meal.

LESSON Be polite and patient when dealing with other people. Libra can't stand crassness.

Flaunt your intelligence

Unlike some astrological signs that are intimidated by high IQs, the Scales value intelligence as much as they crave class. Libra is smart, and needs mental stimulation the way wanderlust Sagittarians need frequent flyer miles.

 LESSON A date with Libra gives you a chance to flaunt your knowledge of obscure art films, Chekhov plays, and last night's *Nova* special without being considered a show-off.

Look good

The question of whether or not you should look your best on a first date is a no-brainer. Go further with Libra, though. Get your hair cut the day before your date, and splurge on a manicure, even if you're a guy going out with a woman.

 LESSON Look especially well groomed for Libra, or Libra will look for someone else.

Be subtle

This advisory is especially important if you two have clicked and you'd like to take things further. Perhaps you want to explore the possibility of sexual seduction. Going to the moon with lovely Libra seems like a possibility.

LESSON Use suggestion to show you're open to a more intimate encounter.

Whatever you do, do it with a figurative (and sometimes literal) light touch. Suggest you share dessert. Brush hands as you both reach for the bread. Saying something like, "How about a quick one?" is the equivalent of pushing your own eject button.

The Libra Deal Breaker: Intellectual Starvation

You're romancing Libra, so shouldn't we be talking about daring deeds done in a gondola? This is a love affair, not a lecture hall. Maybe your love is into sleek cars and doesn't care whether or not mourning becomes Electra. Nevertheless, Libras must be able to connect to their partner mentally, or ultimately the relationship will be brief.

The Committed Relationship: You Got What You Wanted; Here's How to Keep It

The good news about being in a committed relationship with the Scales is that you have someone who wants to be with you, who doesn't expect you to take care of all the household chores (that's what housekeeping services are for), and who will be fair about allocating and sharing assets. Libra isn't fixated on dollar signs, and sees value in intangibles like emotional support. And then there's the active social life. What more could you ask for? Well, you'll certainly get more, whether you ask for it or not.

With all the fringe benefits, there's bound to be a downside. Libras were blessed with tact and cunning that will test your manipulation skills to the utmost. Be agreeable. Traditional astrological dogma says that those guided by this sign couldn't make up their minds to save their lives, much less their relationships. It adds that life isn't all soufflés and nights out on the town. The worst allegation yet is that Libras actually bicker with their mates (insert horrified gasp here).

Libras do tend to go back and forth. It doesn't necessarily mean they're moody, but instead that they're weighing the pros and cons of various situations on their mental scales. Maybe she is thinking about having a circular driveway built. The internal debate goes something like this: "Should it be concrete, like the present driveway, or should it be gravel? Shall I use the contractor the neighbors recommended or look for one on my own? Do I really want a circular driveway? Won't the lot look out of kilter? Will it fit in with the rest of the architecture on the block?" Understand that a furrowed brow means Libra has something on his or her mind. It's not a mood swing. Think of it more as a scale swing.

There's a lot to be said for Libras. There's also a lot to be said *by* them. For the sake of perspective, let's look at Libras outside the romantic realm. You'll see them everywhere, mainly on television. They were born with public-relations credentials. If you switch on the news, and you watch a spokesperson reassuring a nervous public that the city will never go bankrupt, it's a good bet that paragon of poise is a Libra. The Scales are so persuasive, you'll believe their words even though the camera catches the city hall emblem being torn from the wall and moving men snatching the podium out from under the spokesperson's microphone. Remember this: Libras can persuade, finagle, and cajole you into doing anything, because they've been blessed with the gift of persuasion. In a romantic relationship, having only one persuasive person can poison the partnership. It's downright unbalanced and unfair. There's an upside, though: now you can sharpen your manipulative skills, starting with what you know is important to your Libra mate. Here are a few tips on how to use that to keep your relationship as smooth and unruffled as the Scales' own persona.

Emphasize togetherness

Use the term "we" a lot when referring to your partner and yourself. Make sure Libra is within earshot.

Be agreeable

Being agreeable is a pre-emptive strike. Maybe Libra is in the mood for a "lively discussion" (what other people call "a disagreement"). He has taken a stand on an issue such as global warming. The mere mention of that subject on the radio spurs him to say, "Something must be done to prevent it, regardless of the cost."

YOU "I agree."

Libra is at a loss. Where's the fun in having a lively discussion if you agree? Boring! Libra may take the opposite stance just to keep things rolling.

LIBRA "Though it would mean having to get all industrialized countries to consent to taking steps. That would pose both logistical and political problems."

YOU "I agree."

You two could keep this exchange up for hours. But you're dying to sink into your usual hot bath after taking the dog for a walk. So tell your lover:

YOU "I saw a great article on that the other day. Would you like me to find it for you, sweetheart?"

LIBRA (SMILING AT YOUR APPARENT INTEREST IN ENVIRONMENTAL ISSUES AND YOUR CONSIDERATE NATURE) "I'd love it. Shall I run you a bath?"

You stopped the Scales from going back and forth. You also both got what you wanted. There's nothing like mutual consideration. It's enough to make even a pessimist happy.

Be tolerant

You find Libra charming. So do a lot of other people. And Libra does like to circulate, socialize, and yes, even flirt. If you're the jealous type, suppress your reaction—or tip the scales in your own favor by retaliating.

Libra is having a fascinating discussion with one of your colleagues at a company party. Start a fascinating conversation with a very attractive someone else. Considerate as always, Libra checks in with you about a seemingly touchy subject:

LIBRA "I'm going to dance with Frank. You don't mind, do you, darling?"

YOU "Of course not. We were going to take a turn on the dance floor ourselves." Introduce Libra to the very attractive someone else. Then say, "It's a tango." The tango is "your" dance, and the orchestra is playing your song.

LIBRA "Oh."

YOU "See you on the dance floor, dearest."

Libra will still flirt, but at least you reminded her that she's part of a couple. And that you can give as good as you get when it comes to the tactics tango.

Do's and Don'ts in the Libra Mating Game

Do keep the romance alive. You can't expect your mate to do all the work. All it takes is imagination to come up with ways to remind the Scales you love him or her. Draw a heart on a sticky note and affix it to Libra's toothbrush. Put a greeting card underneath the windshield wiper of Libra's car. Leave a message on Libra's voice mail at work so that it's waiting when he or she settles into the office chair first thing in the morning. It will make Libra's day, and maybe your night.

Do consult Libra before you make joint plans. There's nothing your partner enjoys more than being part of a couple. Since Libra is fair, he or she will be happy to split responsibilities down the middle. Let's say you're the designated social planner (as well as the dog walker and car washer). The adept Libra usually has a full social life and always includes you if possible. But in this case, you've connected with a former college professor you'd like to see again. You're afraid Libra will think a physics professor is dull, so be cunning. Use the magic word, "us."

> **YOU** You'll never guess who called me today. *Explain the situation, then top it off with,* "She'd really like to meet us for drinks."
> **LIBRA (REWARDING YOU WITH A SMILE)** Next Saturday works for me. I look forward to it."

Don't let yourself go. Don't get sloppy about your appearance. It's true that Libra was first attracted to your mind, and you haven't stopped being intellectually curious. If you had, Libra would have dumped you by now, or soon will. However, during courtship, Libra was also attracted by your appearance. So, maintain your wardrobe. Continue to wear cologne, and wear sexy underwear to bed. If this gets tiresome, think of the possible fringe benefits.

Don't clutter up Libra's environment. Contrary to pop-culture belief, Libra isn't always the calm, collected embodiment of reason. Scales go up and down, remember? A factor that will cause one side of the scale to plummet and that's guaranteed to wipe the smile off both your faces is an untidy environment. Seeing clutter all the time leaves you so unbalanced. You don't have to be perfect—you're not dealing with a Virgo—but at least be considerate and put away your toys.

You Want Out: Ways to Leave Your Loser

You and Libra were a couple. You lived together, discussed together, and planned a romantic future together. Unfortunately, real life got in the way. You couldn't take any more candlelit dinners, weekend getaways, and florist's bills. Not that you wouldn't like to, but the roof is leaking, the kitchen needs remodeling and with all those three-week jaunts to Paris, your dog is beginning to forget who you are. Libra will be devastated, you think.

You could always try doing things that Libra dislikes, such as:

- Letting yourself go
- Talking with your mouth full
- Interrupting other people while they're speaking
- Forgetting to include Libra's signature on invitations or greeting cards
- Failing to respond to Libra's romantic and intellectual overtures

No, these gambits verge on being childish. Besides, they make you look bad, and you know by contrast how likeable Libra can be. By now, even your oldest friends like him or her more than they like you. You decide you should be forthright and break the sad news that it's time to move on.

Libra will sadly pack up his half of what you've both acquired during the relationship. You're sad, too. But during the move, you notice your new ex is coping quite well, thank you very much. It's because Libras are always in demand and someone else will be happy to take your place. As you watch Libra tape up the last box, you actually see a smile on his face. You guessed it: Libra has a date. Your plan to spend time alone doesn't sound so hot at the moment. As the moving van drives away, you think to yourself, "Hey, that's not fair."

Bliss or Bloodshed: How Your Sign Fits with Libra

♈︎♎︎ **Aries with Libra** See Chapter 1, Libra with Aries.

♉︎♎︎ **Taurus with Libra** See Chapter 2, Libra with Taurus.

♊︎♎︎ **Gemini with Libra** See Chapter 3, Libra with Gemini.

♋︎♎︎ **Cancer with Libra** See Chapter 4, Libra with Cancer.

♌︎♎︎ **Leo with Libra** See Chapter 5, Libra with Leo.

♍︎♎︎ **Virgo with Libra** See Chapter 6, Libra with Virgo.

♎︎♎︎ **Libra with Libra** This same-sign pairing could be like the old movie *Adam's Rib,* in which Katharine Hepburn and Spencer Tracy play married lawyers who find themselves working opposite each other in a sensational attempted-murder case. Talk about bringing work home from the office. The good news is that you're both considerate and understanding. Yes, you crave togetherness, but give each other more space than you'd feel comfortable giving any other sign. The reason is because you both know what your priorities are, jointly and personally, which affords you both a feeling of security. You'll share interests and talk comfortably—frequently. Neither of you is too earthy, unless you have earth planets in your chart, so sex will be light, playful, and fun. There's nothing wrong with this scenario.

♏ ♎ *Scorpio with Libra* Libras shy away from anything too dark and heavy. Some of Scorpio's past experiences might faze a light-spirited and levelheaded Libra. Since the two signs are adjacent to each other in the zodiac, Scorps will often have a planet or two in Libra. This makes them more detached than an undiluted Scorpio. Libra, your chart is probably influenced by the sign of Scorpio. This gives you both chemistry and the ability to relate to each other. Scorpio, take note that apparently easygoing Libra will snap if you hover around and are jealous of everyone Libra befriends. And Libra, your sharp mind will understand that the Scorpion's occasional need to be alone in no way threatens your partnership, nor is it indicative of other romances on the sly. Well, actually, it could be, depending on the Scorpio. They can be saints or sinners, and we've already learned that Libra can go to extremes in an attempt to balance the scales. There's a lot of common ground here. Go play touch football on it—just the two of you.

♐︎ ♎︎   *Sagittarius with Libra* Sadge, you like the way Libra works a room. The two of you might go to a party together, part at the front door, and hook up again only when it's time to go home. However, although Libra likes to circulate, Sagittarius must be sensitive to the Scales' need to be connected. Scope out your mate for an occasional kiss on the neck, or Libra will give you a discourse on manners. If you neglect him or her too much, your partner will find someone who's more attentive. As for you, Libra, Sadge likes your style, but has a problem with what the Archer considers guile. (Most people call it tact, but we'll let the choice of words go for the moment.) Sadge, if Libra can deal with your flightiness, you can stop being so blunt, or at least take it down a notch. Otherwise, this is a harmonious match. You're different superficially, but both of you like to keep things light and fun.

♑︎ ♎︎   *Capricorn with Libra* Both of you are leaders. Capricorns lead in a traditional manner, while Libras are able to accomplish more with a smile and an encouraging word than Capricorn can in a sheaf of executive memorandums. The contrast between communication styles could make for subtle power struggles if you don't watch out. Otherwise, the outlook is sunny. You both appreciate the finer things in life. Cap, you never have to worry that the Scales will let you down. A consummate host or hostess, Libra is one asset you'd like to have on your balance sheet—and your bedsheet. Libra, Capricorn is serious about mating and marrying. You might have to get Capricorn to lighten up occasionally—or frequently. It takes the prodigious skill of a Libra to do that. But if you take a walk down the aisle, you could easily become a power couple. So, have fun together.

♒ ♎ **Aquarius with Libra** The fact that you're air signs indicates that you're both interested in the intellect and can be emotionally detached if the need arises. You'll be friends as well as lovers. Aquarius's tendency to do things in a nontraditional way could make Libra's flesh crawl if taken too far. Water Bearers have been known to wear baseball caps to black tie dinners. It's so embarrassing, isn't it, Libra? Aquarius, be assured you can make an impact without violating dress codes. The two of you will enjoy exchanging ideas. The downside of this match is that it may lack grounding and passion. If it does, and consequently ends, you'll probably remain friends. That's okay though, because you started out as friends, remember?

♓ ♎ **Pisces with Libra** Both of you are considerate and enjoy pleasing other people. You'll be pleased to meet each other. The Fish seems to sense what Libra wants before he or she has to ask for it. One problem here: Pisces isn't the most verbal sign in the zodiac. Fish use sonar and psychic ability to find their way around. Libra, this is no fun when you're up for a lively conversation or need a sounding board. Pisces sees more sides to an issue than you do— which is impressive, given that you can approach an issue from just about any angle. Pisces also has a tendency to shy away from formal partnerships, at least in the beginning. You might have to make do with just living together. So, tuck away your tux or bridal magazines—for now.

8 *the sadistic seducer*

SCORPIO—THE SCORPION OR THE EAGLE, October 24–November 22

♏ SCORPIO'S INTERNET DATING PROFILE

Q: Favorite movie
A: *Mighty Aphrodite*

THE REAL ANSWER: *Apocalypse Now*

Q: Favorite color
A: Burgundy

THE REAL ANSWER: Black. Makes me seem even more mysterious.

Q: Favorite book
A: *The Age of Innocence*

THE REAL ANSWER: *Last Exit to Brooklyn*

Q: Favorite classic song
A: "Don't Get Around Much Anymore"

THE REAL ANSWER: "Let's Do It"

Q: Favorite drink
A: Vintage claret

THE REAL ANSWER: Vintage claret or Perrier. . . or anything that's at least fifty proof.

Q: What is your ideal home?
A: A country home, away from all the city noise. I love the silence.

THE REAL ANSWER: An out-of-the way urban loft, with plush décor that's easily converted into a dungeon-type motif. I love silence (i.e., no communication).

Q: Where will you be in five years?
A: A senior vice president with my current employer.

THE REAL ANSWER: Either the president of my own successful company or in hell.

PS. The posted photo will be current and real, if that's any consolation.

Getting to Know Scorpio

You're in a meadow, standing knee-deep in wildflowers. In the distance you see a knight approach. His horse is black, setting off the silver of his armor and the glint of his sword flapping lightly against his saddle. Maintaining a firm grip on the reigns with one hand, he holds aloft a banner, decorated with his family coat of arms and the Scorpio motto: *Envio Vincere Vici Victum Haud Fides Nothusaum.* Even though you're not wearing flowing robes and a pointy hat, you suddenly feel like a damsel in distress.

The knight jumps gracefully from his horse and sweeps you into his arms, and immediately you're captivated. He's so magnetic that you're enslaved. Literally. Now you're the one who does the sweeping, Cinderella (as well as the dishes and the armor polishing). The next time you lean longingly against this seducer, remember his sword. It's not just for decoration. The Scorpio motto, loosely translated, means: "Conquer and subdue entirely, and never trust the bastards."

 LESSON Beware the Scorpio rescue. It leads to enslavement to his many charms, an abundance of extra housework, and a life that consists of you continually kicking yourself for not paying attention in Latin class.

Maybe you're a guy who's standing in the meadow picking flowers for your girlfriend, and have no desire either to be a damsel or to wear pointy hats. The Scorpio is a maiden who offers to help you pick flowers. She strolls through the meadow, bringing with her the scent of honeysuckle and hot sex. It distracts you from noticing the fabric of her dress, which is patterned with the Scorpio motto. The flowers in your hand are for your now former girlfriend, because you've succumbed to the maiden's charms. And don't bother saying you won't, because you already have. The same inevitability applies after any Scorpio seduction: You'll end up kicking yourself for not paying attention to your Latin teacher.

 LESSON Whether they're male or female, once a Scorpio has scoped you out as a possible partner, you don't stand a chance.

Scorpio in extremis

The thing to remember about all Scorpios is everything about them is extreme—it's black or white, all or nothing, and their vocabulary does not include the word "moderation." Pluto-ruled Scorpio could be a Dorothy Parker wannabe or a trustworthy stockbroker with a stack of disreputable personal secrets. When you make a date with Scorp, you don't know if you'll be transported back in time to the sophistication and wit of the Algonquin Round Table, or end up at a poker party with Tony Soprano at the Bada Bing.

 LESSON Be comfortable going to extremes, or you'll go nowhere with Scorpio.

What's in This Relationship for You

Of course there's something in it for you. Otherwise, Scorpios wouldn't be among the most sought-after signs when it comes to dating, a committed relationship, or at least a quickie. Here's what's included with the Scorpio package:

Sex
Hot, porn-style sex combined with the innocence of a first love.

Depth
Maybe you've been dating a lightweight charmer like Gemini, whose idea of commitment is to send e-mails on a regular basis. If romance were a menu, Scorp would be a welcome chateaubriand when you've been accustomed to ordering only paltry escargot. But wait, there is a slight catch: With such depth as Scorpio's, you might be out of your own depth. This mesmerizer seems so together, you'd never suspect the complicated, fascinating, or downright weird thoughts that swirl through his or her mind. Don't try to peek unless invited. Sometimes ignorance is bliss.

Loyalty
We've all heard about highly sexed Scorpios, and assume there are more notches on their bedpost and more economy-sized boxes of condoms in their bedrooms than in any other sign's. (The notable exception is open-minded Sagittarius, who's so popular and sympathetic. . . . Well, it would've been rude for Sadge to say no, wouldn't it?) Yes, Scorpio does, or did, get around. Which tense to use depends on the phase of life they're currently in. You can bank on one thing, however—once Scorpio has made a commitment to you, you needn't fear betrayal.

How to Attract Scorpio

It's unkind to say that all you have to do to attract a Scorpio is be of the sexually preferred gender and be in the same room. As you've learned from the knight or maiden in the meadow, Scorpio usually chooses his or her paramour. He sees, then seduces, whom he wants. You won't be aware you're even a candidate for the role of Rapunzel or Lancelot, but Scorpio has checked *you* out and wants to haul you off to the castle. Scorpios often do the choosing; they're either completely turned on or completely turned off. An invisible moat surrounds Pluto-ruled people. You'll find either the bridge being lowered for your entrance, or yourself dropped into the water.

 LESSON Unless you've got a taste for pond water that makes a Venetian canal look like a bottle of Evian, let Scorp approach you.

It's always possible to heat things up. If you want, there are ways to attract a Scorpio seducer. Try the following techniques so you can increase your chances of entering Scorpio's magic kingdom.

Dress for sex
You can do so in one of two ways.

Exude Sexuality
Since Scorps think of sex more often than any of the other astrological signs (in other words, twenty-four hours a day), the aroma of sexuality will always snare his attention. Dress to emphasize it. For

example, if you're a woman, show the amount of cleavage that would send conservative Capricorn to check Emily Post's *How to Dress Like a Lady*, or stuffy Taurus to the nearest cardiac unit. A quarter- or half-an-inch will do. Okay, an inch. Much more than that, and Scorpio will still find you sexy, but may also assume you're for hire.

Dress Modestly

Like the conquest junkie Aries, Scorps of either gender crave a challenge. If you seem hard to get (or never gotten), it appeals to Scorpio's love of seduction.

Seeing you across a crowded deli, he senses fresh meat (yes, you, not the pastrami). Scorpio thinks to himself, "This citadel—I mean, deli—will be stormed, and I'm just the person to do it."

There you stand, trying to choose between coleslaw and potato salad, aware you're being checked out. You should be; wearing something that technically is modest but leaves little to the imagination, you've dressed the part. For tips, keep in mind the Gibson-girl idea of proper deportment and dressing: The only skin showing should be that on your face and hands.

Update this ideal to the twenty-first century. For example, wear a turtleneck sweater with a skirt or trousers, and some boots that give the merest hint of style and whiff of sexuality. But the sweater should fit as tightly as possible without your risking a charge of indecent exposure. Or if your asset is your derriere, wear tight slacks. That way, you're technically covered—head to toe—and are therefore irresistibly intriguing to a Scorpio with a yen to conquer virtue.

Whether you decide to go virginal or sexual, wear Scorpio's favorite color: black.

 LESSON To attract Scorpio, appear either virginal or overtly sexual. Your target has a penchant for extremes. Take advantage of it.

If you can manage to look like a virgin and act like a tart in training, or vice versa, you'll intrigue Scorpio even more. You'll be a puzzle, and he is drawn to solving puzzles the way Sherlock Holmes was drawn to a seven-percent solution.

With Scorpio, there are always some imperatives.

The Scorpio Deal Breaker: Infidelity

You'd think such a sensuous person would hold modern views on relationships. You'd be wrong. Have you found a Scorpio who's into sex parties and swapping? Then boink with my blessing. Otherwise, assume that on the subject of fidelity, his outlook is as old-fashioned as a 1950s poodle skirt.

The Committed Relationship: You Got What You Wanted; Here's How to Keep It

You're in love. Now that you've committed to Scorpio and his lusciously wicked ways, here are a few tips to help keep things going.

Be loyal

There's one unforgivable act in Scorpio's book: infidelity. Yes, we've already touched on this, but it bears repeating if you value your life. If Scorpio suspects you of being a side-winding siren, throw him off the scent. Treat him to dinner at his favorite posh restaurant, and perform his favorite sex act, preferably in a public restroom.

Deal with jealousy

If Scorpio thinks you're cheating, it'll take more than bouillabaisse and a blow job to keep you out of trouble. Be prepared to be snooped on at a level unheard of, even at the CIA. Get a replica of your address book and rewrite the entries, leaving out the names of likely suspects (in other words, all the eligible members of the opposite sex). Don't just try to hide your book or he'll think there's something in it that needs hiding, even if there isn't. Cancel caller ID. Whenever possible, turn off your cell phone, a device Scorpio believes was invented for the purpose of making liaisons. Or keep it on, but remember to delete the record of incoming and outgoing calls that he might not approve of.

Accomplish all these steps while acting open and innocent, even—and especially—if you're not.

 LESSON When Scorpio acts jealous, guard your privacy and maintain your dignity. And for God's sake, keep your pants on.

Be alert to control-freak attacks

You're on a routine grocery store run, and as you reach for the Haagen-Dazs, Scorp looks thoughtful, hand on chin, as if considering a major decision.

SCORPIO "Why don't you try Bluebell for a change?"

YOU (THINKING, "I DON'T WANT A CHANGE, I WANT RUM RAISIN") "Why?"

SCORPIO "Well, it has half the amount of fat, and you know I'm watching my cholesterol."

You know he's been watching his cholesterol go down, and there's nothing wrong with his weight or yours.

YOU (AFTER NOTICING THE HAAGEN-DAZS HAPPENS TO BE MORE EXPENSIVE) "Honey, I really have a craving for this, okay?"

SCORPIO (ALSO CRAVING—TO SAVE MONEY AND ESPECIALLY CONTROL BEHAVIOR) "Get whatever you want."

The rest of the day, Scorpio rarely talks to you. You shrug it off, but the sounds of silence stretch into three days. This is called the Scorpio sulk. That disagreement over ice cream at the grocery store was a warning. It wasn't about cholesterol or $1.25. It was about control—Scorp's favorite sport.

Read on to find out how you can keep the issue of control under control.

Nipping Scorpion control-freak attacks in the bud

When a Pluto-ruled person puts his mind to performing a willful act, his discipline rivals that of a monk. Whether Scorp makes a commitment to stop smoking or to waking up at six in the morning even though he's a self-proclaimed night owl, he's just as committed to achieving his goal as he is to you. Unfortunately, control—and unwillingness to let somebody else take charge for a change—is something it would take more than even Merlin and his magic wand to remove from the Scorp psyche.

You may not be Merlin, but you *are* a budding manipulator. Here's how to carve out your share of the Scorpio conglomerate. If she wants control, give it to her.

 LESSON Throw Scorpio a bone to appease her need for control. But choose the bone from an area that isn't important to you.

For example, let's say Scorpio has moved in with you, or you've just gotten a house together. Scorpio has been sulking because you don't like a sculpture she treasures. You've also turned up your nose at the basil seedlings she's cultivating and expressed disdain toward her daffodil bulbs.

To be honest, you aren't interested in decorating or gardening. But let Scorp think you are. Once she's gotten herself into a full-fledged snit, take her hand and say, "I love you and want you to be happy. Mostly, I want you to feel like this is *our* home. I see how important the house and the garden are to you. Do whatever you want with them."

Then let your love decorate the house her way. Put her in charge of planning the herb garden, allow her to pick out the greenhouse of her choice, and let her plant the daffodils anywhere she likes. Be sure, if you value the equipment that fills your trousers, not to interfere.

 LESSON Give Scorpio total control over something, or she'll take total control of you.

Handling the prenup

A prenup is a manifestation of Scorp's desire to control. Even if you're just living together, be prepared and don't freak out when Scorpio whips out a pre-cohabitation agreement. As any Capricorn will tell you, it's wise to cover your investments, as well as your ass, in any committed relationship. Maybe you don't yet have a pricey house, a Hummer, or a stack of Krugerrands accumulating in a bank vault. But you're in—or about to be in—a committed relationship. Tune out unkind people (in other words, those who've already dated Scorpios) who say you'll wish you'd been committed to an institution instead. Just think of all of your lover's good points. Not making an issue out of the prenup fools Scorp into thinking you're a pushover, and protects your assets at the same time. Meanwhile, secretly get a good lawyer to look it over before you sign.

Do's and Don'ts in the Scorpio Mating Game

Do be available.
Do be sexual.

Do be open-minded.
Do be deep.
Don't flirt with other people.

Don't act silly. Dignity is as important to Scorpio as cash is to Capricorn.

Don't lie to anyone. Scorpios assume if you lie to somebody else, you'll lie to them. And what happens if you lie to Scorp? Well, for an idea of the consequences of that scenario, watch any episode of *CSI* or read the works of Stephen King.

You Want Out: Ways to Leave Your Loser

Well, it hasn't worked out, after all. After an argument, Scorpio yanked up your flower bulbs just as they had started to grow. You want to be shallow for a change, and you're sick of being under surveillance. The hot sex has cooled off as far as your needs are concerned, but you're still being asked to perform twice a day. You're tired of endless devotion, and want to explore pursuing a lightweight date with one or even all of the other astrological signs.

There are usually many ways to leave a loser. Unfortunately, with a still-devoted Scorpio, there is only one:

Change your name and leave the state.

Bliss or Bloodshed: How Your Sign Fits with Scorpio

♈ ♏ **Aries with Scorpio** See Chapter 1, Scorpio with Aries.

♉ ♏ **Taurus with Scorpio** See Chapter 2, Scorpio with Taurus.

♊ ♏ **Gemini with Scorpio** See Chapter 3, Scorpio with Gemini.

♋ ♏ **Cancer with Scorpio** See Chapter 4, Scorpio with Cancer.

♌ ♏ **Leo with Scorpio** See Chapter 5, Scorpio with Leo.

♍ ♏ **Virgo with Scorpio** See Chapter 6, Scorpio with Virgo.

♎ ♏ **Libra with Scorpio** See Chapter 7, Scorpio with Libra.

♏ ♏ **Scorpio with Scorpio** Considering you're both into control, Scorpios get along surprisingly well with their own kind. Each of you is comfortable swimming in the depths of the human psyche and can quote Freud and Baudelaire at the drop of a condom. Most importantly, you understand the importance of passion, as anyone with a brain or an age in the double digits should. You'll either be instantly attracted to each other, or instantly at war. So, if you do pair up, the best way to get along is to understand you both have power. If one of you tries to outmuscle the other, you're in trouble. Recognize that you've met your match, and aim for a balance of power. After all, it worked during the Cold War.

♐ ♏ **_Sagittarius with Scorpio_** On the plus side, you're both explorers, Scorpio of the psyche and Sadge of the world. On the negative side, Sagittarians like to explore everything, including other lovers. Scorpios won't stand for that. So, Archer, there's one of two ways this relationship could turn out: You could get Scorpio to lighten up a little by your example, or Scorpio could show you that it can be darkest after as well as before the dawn. But you're both knowledgeable, and can carry on long philosophical conversations (preferably in your favorite bars). As Sagittarius, you're a bit of a gambler and even with the odds, you'll probably give this one a whirl. If it doesn't work out, you're good at turning former lovers into friends, which sometimes works with Scorpio. You have another advantage over the other signs: With all those frequent flyer miles, if need be you can make a quick getaway.

♑ ♏ **_Capricorn with Scorpio_** Ambition—you both understand it and encourage each other to go for it. Surprisingly, Capricorn, you and your mate won't be competing with one another. Scorpio is quiet about his or her goals, while your drive is out in the open (but tastefully so). One trouble spot could be that you're both so single-mindedly ambitious that you let the romance die. You'll know you're in trouble if Scorpio no longer approaches you sexually. If this happens, wake up fast and start doing your duty. Once Scorpio has lost all passion, it's as hard to restore as a good credit rating.

♒ ♏ **_Aquarius with Scorpio_** We can simply call this one a war of the worlds. Aquarius, your world is one in which everyone has equality under the law and a politically correct diet, and wears clothes made from only natural fibers. You espouse these views proudly and publicly. Unfortunately, you tend to expect your lover to do the same. Scorpio's world is based on personal independence and privacy. The Scorpion may share your political views but frowns on your way of expressing them. Scorp wields power from behind the scenes and won't take kindly to being looked down on because he or she won't go to a rally or carry a sign on a stick. Worse, if you foist dietary rules on your lover, she will refuse outright. (How *dare* you try to control what she wants to eat?!) You can imagine what all this friction will do to your day-to-day romance, not to mention your sex life. There is common ground here: You both need to decide where you can compromise. If you can't, neither of you will be saying "I do." Instead, you'll bid *adieu*.

♓♏ **Pisces with Scorpio** Good match, great chemistry. Each of you is emotional and empathetic, and will feel a connection right away. After you bond, you'll both disappear for a while, and friends will wonder where you are. The answer: in bed. Also, you both like mystery and secrecy. Don't take the secrecy too far, Pisces, or Scorp will think you're up to something. You may be occupied with perfectly harmless activities during all those hours you can't account for, but your mate will jump to the conclusion that you're being unfaithful. This suspicion brings out the Sherlock in Scorpio, which is always a bad move with Pisces. You hate being under surveillance so much that you'd be willing to walk away from love and great sex. Advice to you, Scorpio: trust the Fish until you have concrete evidence of infidelity. It would be a shame to waste all those condoms.

9 *the absentee admirer*

SAGITTARIUS—THE ARCHER,
November 23–December 21

Q: Favorite movie
A: *Alfie.* Now that's an adventure story.

THE REAL ANSWER: *Out of Africa.* It has adventure, travel, exotic animals, and hunting trips. I like travel, not hunting trips because I like animals, but. . . . [Note to reader: Sagittarius has exceeded the space limit.]

Q: Favorite color
A: Orange. It's cheerful.

THE REAL ANSWER: Any color. They're all fine, but beige is nice because it looks like sand, and white is good 'cause it reminds me of clouds when I'm looking out the window of an airplane, and . . . .[Note to reader: Sagittarius has exceeded the space limit again.]

Q: Favorite book
A: *The Accidental Tourist*—cool name for a book. It sounded really fun but it turned out to be about somebody who hated traveling and it was darker than I expected it to be. I guess I was an accidental reader.

THE REAL ANSWER: *West With the Night* or north, south, or east, so I can get away in the dark if my quickie starts to turn into clingy commitment.

Q: Favorite classic song
A: "When You're Smiling"

THE REAL ANSWER: "Born to Run"

Q: Favorite drink
A: Anything as long as it's big but will fit into my backpack if I bother to carry one.

THE REAL ANSWER: Something that will make me fly even if I'm sitting in an armchair.

Q: What is your ideal home?
A: An apartment. I have fake plants so they'll always look good as new, no matter how long I'm gone.

THE REAL ANSWER: A tent. It'll feature several secret entrances. It's kinda like I'm playing Valentino or vamp extraordinaire Theda Bara. And my tent will have emergency escape flaps so nobody gets their feelings hurt.

Q: Where will you be in five years?
A: Who knows? Some people say I'll be in court, running neck and neck with Gemini in the multiple-exes race.

THE REAL ANSWER: On the move and still having fun.

Getting to Know Sagittarius

Imagine the magnificent centaur. This mythical creature, half man and half horse, is something to behold. In his masculine, muscular arms, he carries a quiver of arrows that he shoots high into the air while running as fast as his four legs will go. With high expectations and firm fetlocks, the Archer shoots at many targets. You will be one of them. Sadge is always on the alert for fresh game.

Sagittarius, the Archer, is symbolized by the Centaur. Sagittarians are optimistic, frank, adventurous, and extremely likable. Yet there's a puzzling paradox here, as anyone who's been romantically involved with a Sadge can tell you. All of the astrological signs have two sides: evolved and prehistoric. Yes, the Sagittarian sunny, funny optimism is a constant. But the Archer's eagerness to explore can lead him or her into overdrive. Sometimes he will connect with new people while hooked up with you. Then the normally frank, aboveboard Sagittarius can out-sneak Pisces, out-lie Gemini, and out-lay Scorpio. Don't be angry. Remember, a Centaur is half man and half beast. And unfortunately, the Archer can't help that his lower half is all beast.

What's in This Relationship for You

Many perks come standard with the Sagittarian relationship; in fact, they're as numerous as Sadge's past lovers. Here are a few examples.

Positivity

An Archer can banish a case of the glooms with his or her mere presence. His positive outlook will rub off on anyone, even an arch

150   Astrologically Incorrect for *lovers*

pessimist like Capricorn. But some negatives stem from constantly consorting with such an extremely positive person. It's great as long as a sunny outlook doesn't degenerate into wishful thinking or cloud your common sense. If your sole desire were for life to be like a Frank Capra film, you'd invest in a Capra Classics Collection, which includes *It's a Wonderful Life* and *Mr. Smith Goes to Washington.* You could stay home, set the DVD menu to "continuous play," and order pizza in every night. It would save plenty of money you'd otherwise spend on dates.

 LESSON Beware of relentless positivism. Strike a balance by remembering to accentuate the negative.

Optimism

Optimism is another trait that is included in the Sadge package. It can be so refreshing, especially if you've just gotten out of a relationship with a nagging nitpicker who was impossible to please. Imagine you're on your way to an outdoor concert with Sadge. Tickets in hand, you're about to dash out the door when a thought suddenly occurs.

YOU "Shall we bring a blanket in case the ground is damp?"

SADGE "No, it's a long walk from the parking lot. We don't want to carry extra stuff." You see the point and grab just a light jacket. Sadge continues, "Why do you need a jacket? It's a balmy night."

YOU "Yeah, but the weather forecast said temperatures are going to drop. There might even be a light drizzle."

SADGE (LOOKING AT YOU INDULGENTLY) "You're so cute, believing in weather forecasts. Let's go."

YOU (HANGING ONTO YOUR JACKET AND FOLLOWING THE ARCHER TO THE CAR) "Yes, but even a meteorologist is right at least half the time."

Jazzed about the upcoming musical evening, Sadge hums a few tunes while driving. You arrive at the venue, find a place to sit, and settle in. Is the ground damp? Yes. Does the temperature drop? Uh-huh. Does a light rain fall from the sky? You guessed it, although you would never stoop to saying, "I told you so." Through chattering teeth, Sadge admits, "You were right." There's nothing like an admission of impracticality to impress a person. So you say only, "Scoot closer and we'll hold my jacket over our heads." What else can you do with such a good sport?

Popularity

Can you handle the horrors of having a popular mate? Chances are, any time you're out with an Archer, someone else will know him or her. You could be at the grocery store, an arts festival, or a home improvement shop and Sadge will run into a friend or acquaintance. He'll run into trouble by engaging in conversation, reminiscences, and the exchange of updated e-mail addresses while totally ignoring you. He doesn't mean to be rude; he's just being himself. If you like staying close to your date while at a social function, you'll be disappointed. At a party, Sadge will say something like, "I'll get you a drink and be right back." After an hour or so has passed and you're still thirsty and without escort, you realize your definition of "right back" is different from Sadge's. Sadge doesn't mean to be inattentive, or intend anything devious by adding new e-mail addresses to his little black book. But he *is* absent and probably *will* augment the black book.

 LESSON If Sadge sets you adrift on a date, it's not out of maliciousness—but rather, it's the price you pay for the delightful life you'll lead with a Sagittarius.

How to Attract Sagittarius

Be realistic

You're a perceptive person and probably have already picked up on the fact that it's easy to attract a Sadge. His gregariousness, adventurousness, and utter disinterest in considering the consequences of his actions make the Archer one of the most experienced signs of the zodiac. With all his vast experience, the Archer has quite a past.

Do you want to get involved with such a Don Juan? You think of Sadge's good points, but as you do so, you can't help but think of all the lovers who came before you. Wouldn't it be fun to get the lowdown from his exes on what Sadge really likes and what life would be like with him? You imagine getting them together at a party and quizzing them. So, we're going to use a peek inside his little black book to conjure up an imaginary party for Sagittarius's former flames. Here's your chance to learn from experience, even someone else's. In this case, we'll assume you're interested in a Sagittarian guy. But you can reverse the gender, and the principle remains the same.

Be ready to meet Sadge's exes

The first to ring your doorbell is a cool vision in white. You're reminded of black-and-white movies, Lana Turner in a clinch with John Garfield, and James M. Cain novels. You've heard that the postman always rings twice. This dame is so glamorous, you're certain she's never had to ring more than once. She saunters into your living room and says, "Hi, I was married to Sadge for a while. Do you have an ashtray?"

As you provide one, you wonder how quickly you can get an appointment at Elizabeth Arden. It looks like Sadge is out of your league.

Then the next ex arrives. You're astonished: She's an attractive intellectual type who would look at home in front of any university classroom. "Hello. Thanks for the invitation. I dated Sagittarius after my second divorce."

You get ex Number Two settled, and steel yourself for the next arrival. Will she be a ballerina or a bartender? She's neither—she's down-to-earth.

"Hi, girls," she says as she joins the other two guests. The glamour queen asks, "How's the dog breeding going? You must come to see me when you're in town for the Westminster Kennel Club Dog Show."

They're all chatting with each other. Then the academic turns to you. "I imagine you want to know what he's like."

After you admit that indeed you would, they start talking.

Ex Number Two proclaims, "We met through Sadge. We're all friends."

Visions of kinky arrangements enter your head as Ex Number Three adds, "Yes, but not intimate friends, if you know what I mean. And we're still on good terms with Sadge."

Taken aback, you say, "But that's so odd. It means the Archer must have treated each of you really well. So why did you split up?"

Ex Number One pipes up, "He charged a gift to his girlfriend on our joint credit card."

Ex Number Two adds, "He always planned vacations during the academic year when I couldn't go with him."

Ex Number Three murmurs sheepishly, "He lost interest."

You say uncertainly, "But I don't detect any bitterness here."

The women chime in unison, "He always stayed in touch and is such a good friend!"

As the exes depart, you ponder the information you've just been given. The Archer doesn't seem to have a particular "type." It's not his fault that he's had a multitude of past romances. At least he doesn't claim that the failed relationships were all *their* fault.

 LESSON There's no need to worry about whether you're tall enough, have the preferred hair color, or work in the correct profession. Open-minded Sadge will give a relationship with you a whirl. This is great for your ego—at least at first.

The Sagittarius Deal Breaker: Clinginess

A Sagittarius is the wrong choice for you if you require his or her constant reassurance or presence. Maintain an active social life of your own and lean on your friends if you need. Archers find clingy behavior off-putting, even in someone they love.

The Committed Relationship: You Got What You Wanted; Here's How to Keep It

As you've undoubtedly already gleaned from this chapter, amusement and excitement are in store for you in the company of a Sagittarius. Now that you've jumped into a relationship with sunny Sadge, be mindful that it can turn out one of two ways. It could be like opening a Fabergé egg and discovering a chirping robin. Or you could bite into the golden apple only to find it's all skin and no fruit. Whether your union with the Archer will resemble the Fabergé egg or the poisoned apple depends on the stage of life where your mate is. If he or she is young, expect to have a great time but don't get too attached. If Sadge has been around the block—or the globe— chances are there will be fewer problems with commitment issues.

Read on to find out how you can trick Sadge into thinking the practicalities of real life are fun.

Be spontaneous

Call Sagittarius in the middle of the day and suggest she skip her power lunch to meet you in the park for a picnic.

Be low maintenance

Shrug it off if the Archer gets home late from work, and refrain from scolding him if he forgets to call to let you know he'll be delayed. Just order takeout or go out. Sagittarius will be happy you're independent. After a while, though, he'll realize you don't need him. Don't be surprised if he starts coming home early and sending flowers with the ardor of a teenager who's found his first love.

Get used to frankness

Learn to embrace tactlessness. Sadge has all the best intentions in the world, but sometimes forgets to soften comments. Imagine you're out shopping with Sadge and you both encounter a Piscean friend.

SADGE "Hi, it's great to see you. I heard you got into trouble with sticky fingers in a department store, but that now you pay for stuff. And you even work in retail. Oh, this is your boss? Sorry."

SADGE (TURNING HIS ATTENTION TO THE EMPLOYER IN QUESTION) "You've got a great employee here. Not only does Pisces really know his stock, but he also has an instinct for how to hide it in his jeans so that it's invisible—even that $400 lampshade that was in the shop window last week. And the only time he'll be late is when he remembers he has a job."

Then Sadge laughs and says his goodbyes. What he doesn't realize is this time will be his last with his Pisces friend.

This is an extreme example, but you get the idea. Yours will be the unlucky lot of diplomatically helping to defuse potentially explosive situations.

Do's and Don'ts in the Sagittarius Mating Game

Do share the Archer's liking for adventure. Be ready to travel at a moment's notice.

Do keep things light emotionally. Let your depth sneak up later.

Don't make references to a long-term relationship. Not at the beginning, at least. If you say things like "we" and "next year" too soon, a Sagittarius will find the nearest airport.

Don't get upset when Sagittarius contacts ex-lovers. They are friends, remember? It's the folks Sadge hasn't met yet who may be cause for worry.

You Want Out: Ways to Leave Your Loser

Sagittarius wasn't ready for you, or you weren't ready for Sagittarius. Your frequent flyer miles are used up and so is your patience. Sagittarius feels smothered. It's time to put this relationship out of its misery.

You could develop a fascination with fine china patterns and the engagement-announcement section of the newspaper, and drop hints about diamond rings hefty enough to put Liz Taylor's collection to shame. This will frighten a commitment-phobe immediately.

Another, more expedient, option is simply to say, "You know, this really isn't working. Friends?" Thankfully, Sadge will answer, "Friends." Now you're officially one of the exes, and have gained a whole new group of friends.

Bliss or Bloodshed: How Your Sign Fits with Sagittarius

♈ ♐ **Aries with Sagittarius** See Chapter 1, Sagittarius with Aries.

♉ ♐ **Taurus with Sagittarius** See Chapter 2, Sagittarius with Taurus.

♊ ♐ **Gemini with Sagittarius** See Chapter 3, Sagittarius with Gemini.

♋ ♐ **Cancer with Sagittarius** See Chapter 4, Sagittarius with Cancer.

♌ ♐ **Leo with Sagittarius** See Chapter 5, Sagittarius with Leo.

♍ ♐ **Virgo with Sagittarius** See Chapter 6, Sagittarius with Virgo.

♎ ♐ *Libra with Sagittarius* See Chapter 7, Sagittarius with Libra.

♏ ♐ *Scorpio with Sagittarius* See Chapter 8, Sagittarius with Scorpio.

♐ ♐ *Sagittarius with Sagittarius* Same-sign matches always have built-in pluses and minuses. On the plus side, both of you shoot for the moon in every area of life. Now you're with someone who won't pooh-pooh your wild ideas to master mountain climbing even though neither of you has ever tried it. Before you know it, maps, plane schedules, and mountain-climbing-gear catalogs will be spread out all over your dining room table. The appropriate classes are signed up for and travel plans have been made. But you've hit a snag: Neither of you thought about how to finance the trip, request time off from work, or cancel newspaper delivery for the time you'll be gone. Being optimistic, you two decide to start over and factor in those pesky details. The challenge here is for both of you to be practical—at least occasionally. Then you can have a great time with those brilliant ideas.

♑ ♐ *Capricorn with Sagittarius* Sagittarians and Capricorns are very different. Capricorn, before taking a chance, you carefully weigh pros and cons and make a decision after plenty of time has passed. Sagittarius, you weigh the pros and cons, check the odds, discover they're nearly insurmountable, and go for it regardless. Who wants the boredom of a sure thing? Well, Capricorn does. After all, it's not boring, it's practical. The real challenge in this romance is that when Sadge looks on the bright side, Capricorn thinks the Archer is wearing blinders. And when the Goat is being prudent, Sadge sees him or her as a pessimist. Eventually, the grinding together of these two different perspectives could wear down Sadge's confidence. Try to learn from instead of changing each other. Sagittarius, you'll take a chance. Capricorn, how about you?

♒ ♐ *Aquarius with Sagittarius* This pairing makes for easy sailing. Both of you are freewheeling types who respect each other's privacy. You're also both very independent and self-sufficient. Sexual vibes between you are good, and you're likely to enjoy an unconventional sex life. However, a Sagittarius-Aquarius relationship is likely to end with indifference rather than a big blowout. Just make sure you stay connected and pay attention to each other. Otherwise, you may wake up one day and find you've transformed from lovers into just friends.

♓ ♐ *Pisces with Sagittarius* On the positive side, each of you is flexible. The downside of this match has its roots in the differences between the ways you both think. Sadge, you make quick decisions and talk freely, although not always tactfully. Intuitive Pisces soaks up the moods of people and places around him or her. Needless to say, Fishes are sensitive. Comments tossed out carelessly by the Archer land on Pisces like harpoons. The problem is that Pisceans, who rarely complain, will withdraw. Unfortunately, Sadges assume everything is okay unless told it isn't. Pisces, learn how to say "ouch," and Sadge, make an effort to soften your comments. Or skip it all, and just go for a light sex fling. It all depends on how much chemistry is present and how much you're both willing to work on potential problems.

10 *the potentate of protocol*

CAPRICORN—THE GOAT,
December 22–January 20

♑ CAPRICORN'S INTERNET DATING PROFILE

Q: Favorite movie
A: *The Philadelphia Story*

THE REAL ANSWER: *The Philadelphia Story*

Q: Favorite color
A: Green

THE REAL ANSWER: Green paper decorated with pictures of presidents.

Q: Favorite book
A: *Brideshead Revisited*

THE REAL ANSWER: *Brideshead Revisited*

Q: Favorite classic song
A: "My Funny Valentine"

THE REAL ANSWER: "Love for Sale"

Q: Favorite drink
A: Chateau Lafitte, any vintage

THE REAL ANSWER: Chateau Lafitte 1961, when it's someone else's turn to pay the bar tab.

Q: What is your ideal home?
A: A comfortable home in a community with a low crime rate and good schools. Safety comes first. If that means high property taxes, it's worth it for the comfort and safety of those I love.

THE REAL ANSWER: A comfortable home that's a five-minute walk from my office building. Or one that's actually in my office building. Either had better have low property taxes or I'll contest the property appraisal.

Q: Where will you be in five years?
A: In a stable job environment with a good record of advancement and in a stable committed relationship.

THE REAL ANSWER: Running in exalted professional and social circles. Candidate for the "romantic mate" position had better own a ladder: I'm using mine.

P.S. Capricorn's posted photograph will be authentic. It will also have been taken by a professional photographer, not some amateur with a digital camera.

Getting to Know Capricorn

You're looking for love in most of the right places, using a dating service, taking a friend's recommendation, and saying nightly novenas. And what have you gotten for your trouble? More trouble: a Pisces who was so tuned into you that he disappeared just when needed, a Sagittarius who gave you Pollyanna pep talks about personal devotion while jumping on a plane, and a Gemini who eloquently expressed his undying love after he'd already buried it.

Where are the lovers of substance? How do you find someone who'll be there for you whenever you call? Who will wrap you in sexy security, not to mention sexy securities? Maybe you weren't looking in the right places after all. Try tapping into another source by closely examining the people around you in your office lobby.

You spot Capricorn. Dressed in traditional business attire and carrying a briefcase, at first he or she resembles the other people who catch a commuter train at the same time each morning. It isn't the first time you've seen this Goat. You remember thinking he has all the warmth of a nuclear winter and is as full of laughs as a poem by Sylvia Plath. You can't imagine such a person taking off his clothes, much less having sex.

Then you look more closely, and sense that beneath the corporate disguise is a good-looking individual who can close a deal and open a bedroom door. As you mentally dump the nonstarters, you feel like you've found fifty thousand dollars in the old cookie jar Grandmother left you. Congratulations on seeing past Capricorn's façade. Comfort yourself with your success now, because you'll still have to penetrate that façade later.

What's in This Relationship for You

Finally, you've found someone you can bring home to your mother; even the nitpickiest Mom is sure to approve of Cap. What other goodies are in store for you?

Quality over quantity

There are many credits in Capricorn's ledger of romance. You've found someone who'll keep you warm at night by wrapping you in a blanket made of cashmere instead of synthetic fiber. You will be taken to the best restaurants and have season tickets to the opera along with new opera glasses. You'll also seldom see your lover before 11 P.M. on workdays. Wait a minute—that doesn't sound very romantic. How can you cuddle up to Capricorn when he or she's working long hours? Welcome to the debit side of the Goat's romantic ledger.

Yin and yang

Capricorns come in many guises. That of corporate crusader is only one. Add the following to the list: the socialite (or social register wannabe), ruthless boss, and workaholic. There's no need to go into the last entry on that list, because the description is true of all Goats. Let's examine the socialite and ruthless boss personas. As you know, every astrological sign has an enlightened side and an unevolved side. First, let's take a walk on the lighter side.

Imagine it's 1939 and you're on the set of a black-and-white movie. George Cukor is directing a scene in which Katharine Hepburn is dancing with Jimmy Stewart. Their characters have imbibed enough champagne to make them light on their feet and even lighter in the head. Slight inebriation leads them to lose their inhibitions and loosen their tongues. Dropping their masks, both talk to each other as equals. Welcome to *The Philadelphia Story*. This is style untouched by "trendiness," good taste without ostentation. Cukor's cinematic concoction depicts the best side of a socially oriented Goat. But there's one more type of Goat to visit. Let's jump back in time to the late 1920s. Again, dancing and champagne surrounds you. But the pace is frenzied and the people seem reckless. Then you understand why: You're in a speakeasy, where the only thing prohibited is Prohibition. Why is everyone so nervous? They're antsy because this joint is owned by mobster supreme Al Capone. Let's travel back to the present before Valentine's Day arrives, and the massacre–even in his absence—along with it.

Now you've witnessed the light side and the dark depths of Capricorn's nature. What will the relationship with the Goat you met be like: Cukor or Capone? A little of each, probably, which is what could make it exciting.

How to Attract Capricorn

As grievous as it may be to say, you face a teensy-weensy barrier when you decide to approach Capricorn. The Goat is emotionally guarded and unlikely to warm up to you until after you've opened up first. It's emotionally a "money-up-front" situation: You must pay admission before you're allowed to enter. In the face of this new challenge, your knee-jerk reaction is probably, "It's not fair," mainly because it isn't. All that was required to attract Sadge was to be sociable and in the same room. With Pisces, you simply needed to accentuate your spiritual side and be a shameless tease. And to attract Gemini, you just had to know the latest news headlines and feign lightheartedness. So why must you undertake the emotional equivalent of stripping yourself bare while the Goat gets to wear a mask? There are two reasons.

Realize that Capricorn is cautious

Relationships require investments of time, energy, and emotion. And Capricorn is very protective of investments.

 LESSON Whether Cap is choosing a barbecue pit, a new lawn mower, or a mate, he'll consider things carefully before he makes an investment.

Capricorn takes commitment seriously

When considering embarking on a new relationship, the Goat makes projections about your joint future. You've already been imagined as a parent to future children, a partner in entertaining business associates, and a companion in retirement.

 LESSON When Capricorn makes a commitment, he sticks to it. That's why he takes his time before entering into one.

The Capricorn Seduction

Unkind souls assert that the words "Capricorn" and "seduction" don't belong in the same sentence. But go talk to someone who's consummated a business deal with Capricorn, and you'll discover the Goat is capable of shameless seduction. This is one serious suitor, so be prepared: He or she will use those same skills to seduce you romantically. The following scenario will give an idea of what this feels like.

Imagine a normal day at work. While you're walking down the corridor, you feel as if you're being watched. Did you miss a meeting? Is your boss annoyed? You try to shake off this feeling after work while you return your library books, pick up your dry cleaning, and grab Thai takeout for dinner. Are you paranoid? You credit having read a thriller the night before with your heightened sensitivity, and then forget about your suspicions.

But the next day you have the same feeling at the office. What's going on? Capricorn has been watching you with the skill and secrecy of a CIA agent. He or she's assessing your potential. The Goat wants to see if you make the cut before spending wasted time with you. The next thing you know, Cap will ask you out to dinner.

 LESSON If Capricorn approaches you, you've already taken a step up the ladder. Funny, you didn't know you were climbing one.

Now that you've been asked to dine with the Goat, it's time to turn the tables. Cap dislikes overtly aggressive types, so here's your chance to have fun by being passive aggressive. Although both you and the Goat know you're there to be checked out, make no mention of it. Keep the conversation as light as a soufflé. Remember, be the first to let your guard down—but reveal just enough to keep the Goat interested. The following tactics will get you past the first date and on to the next one. If you want to continue, that is.

Dress elegantly

Does your idea of dressing up mean flashy clothes? Instead, wear an ensemble that appears plain yet cost almost as much as your car did. If that's out of your price range, choose something simple but add expensive accents. Toss aside the junk jewelry in favor of genuine pearls, or if you're a guy, your onyx cuff links.

Demonstrate your linguistic skills

Your dinner partner made reservations in advance, so use the time before your date to sneak a peek at the menu and wine list. The restaurant can probably fax a copy to you. If you can't pronounce Pouilly-Fuissé or steak *au poivre,* learn how.

 LESSON Capricorn is impressed by people who don't have to resort to ordering their wine by pointing at the list.

Be courteous

Capricorn will do everything the proper way, with good manners. The Goat expects you to show good manners, too.

 LESSON If you open a door and stride through it first, you've taken a step down the ladder.

The Capricorn Deal Breaker: Irresponsibility

This kind of behavior is intolerable to the Goat. Respect your elders, get to the office on time, and stash cash in an easily accessible place in case of emergency. You won't have to use it, of course, because Cap will not allow emergencies to happen. (Yeah, right . . . and people say Capricorns are realistic. Emergencies do happen.)

The Committed Relationship: You Got What You Wanted; Here's How to Keep It

If Capricorn is interested in you, commitment is almost a certainty, once you've passed the background and credit checks. So, you've made the cut and are officially in the Goat's life. Caution: Yes, Capricorns have flings, but most of them aspire to being in a committed relationship. If your idea of commitment is calling Cap once or twice a week and meeting for dinner as time allows, you're better off with another sign. When the Goat is part of the picture, engraved invitations, flounced dresses, and rented tuxedos are called for. No, Capricorn doesn't want to go to the prom—he or she wants to get married. Can you deal with the horror of living such a stable, predictable life? If the thought frightens you, remember there's a little Capone in every Capricorn. Other admirable qualities befitting a spouse can be found in your mate. Here are a couple.

Trustworthiness

You've heard much about Capricorn's dependability. Then something happens that makes you wonder if the Goat is being sneaky.

He claims to be working, but you discover he's playing golf. Later, you hear about a conference that is to be held in Bangkok. "Aha," you think, "classic alibi for someone who's having an affair." Before you retain a lawyer, delve deeper. Cap *is* working. The Goat puts in time at the office but knows he'll advance faster if he also shows clients or associates a good time.

 LESSON If the Goat says he's working, it means he's working.

Predictability

If Capricorn is going to be late, she will call to let you know. Unfortunately, Capricorn can also be predictable when it comes to sex. This activity has quite possibly been written into the domestic schedule. Imagine a list that says: rake the leaves, regrout the kitchen tile, clean the carpet, have sex, do the dishes, and change the sheets. Isn't it romantic? Oddly enough, Capricorn has a reputation for being cold. Actually, the Goat is quite earthy and very much likes sex, as long as it doesn't involve surprises. Ignore the set "schedule," but approach your lover sexually in the proper manner—meaning, in the bedroom. If you want to get laid, avoid seducing Cap while he or she's preoccupied with business matters. At that time, it's a business rival he's thinking about screwing, not you.

Do's and Don'ts in the Capricorn Mating Game

Do be discreet.

Do be alert for sighs. Excessive sighing is Capricorn's way of letting you know how heavy the load is, and how dutiful he or she is. You detect the odor of burning martyr. Note the sighs, then ignore them.

Don't get on his bad side. Capricorn's steady nature is so appealing, you'll think there is no bad side, only a boring one. But remember—there's more to your partner than you suspect. Before you met Cap, yearning for excitement, you took a chance and ran off with someone who was mad, bad, and dangerous to know. But now you've wised up . . . or have you? Capricorn may not be mad, but otherwise, the same description applies. Don't mess with the Goat.

Don't be late. This is disrespectful and irresponsible. We already know how Cap reacts to that.

You Want Out: Ways to Leave Your Loser

You simply cannot stand this life any longer. The Goat is prodding you into planning your retirement and you're only twenty years old. Or maybe you couldn't compete with the ultimate rival: Capricorn's career. What happened to the elegance of *The Philadelphia Story* referred to earlier? The Goat must have left it in San Francisco while there on business. Not even the dangerous allure of Cap's Capone side surfaces often enough to tempt you into staying. As far as you're concerned, it's over.

The easiest way to ditch a Capricorn is to embarrass him or her in public. Of course, you'll embarrass yourself as well, so try something else.

Act irresponsible

Tell Capricorn that you're pretending to be sick and will take a week off from work. You're actually using legitimate vacation time, but he or she doesn't have to know. Forget to turn on the sprinklers, wash the dishes, re-grout the kitchen tile, and change the sheets. Watch trash television. Buy a subscription to a tacky gossip rag and have it sent to Capricorn's office address.

If you did get sucked into marriage, call your lawyer. If you're low on money, use cash from Capricorn's emergency fund. The Goat won't miss it for a while. Remember, in Capricorn's world, there *are* no emergencies.

Bliss or Bloodshed: How Your Sign Fits with Capricorn

♈ ♑ *Aries with Capricorn* See Chapter 1, Capricorn with Aries.

♉ ♑ *Taurus with Capricorn* See Chapter 2, Capricorn with Taurus.

♊ ♑ *Gemini with Capricorn* See Chapter 3, Capricorn with Gemini.

♋ ♑ *Cancer with Capricorn* See Chapter 4, Capricorn with Cancer.

♌ ♑ **Leo with Capricorn** See Chapter 5, Capricorn with Leo.

♍ ♑ **Virgo with Capricorn** See Chapter 6, Capricorn with Virgo.

♎ ♑ **Libra with Capricorn** See Chapter 7, Capricorn with Libra.

♏ ♑ **Scorpio with Capricorn** See Chapter 8, Capricorn with Scorpio.

♐ ♑ **Sagittarius with Capricorn** See Chapter 9, Capricorn with Sagittarius.

♑ ♑ **Capricorn with Capricorn** Two Capricorns can build a grand life together. However, there will be power struggles, since both of you are used to being in charge. Rather than being overtly competitive, each of you will try to out-achieve the other. This could lead to either affluence or early coronaries. One of you will need to remind the other that there's more to life than duty and work. Take walks together, go to hockey games, or find other fun activities. (Perhaps you should call a Sagittarius for suggestions should you get stuck.) If the relationship goes sour, both of you will work hard to restore its sweetness. Now, that's a job well done.

♒ ♑ **Aquarius with Capricorn** Aquarians may act loopy, but behind the façade they're smart. Capricorns appreciate excellence, especially intellectual. But you don't like unpredictability, do you, Capricorn? Aquarians thrive on acting on a whim and stirring up the pot. The idea of overtly thumbing one's nose at the status quo gives Goats the shivers. There is a side to Aquarius, though, that enables you to relate to Capricorn's sense of duty. But the rebellious hell-raiser within you will challenge your mate constantly. The more conservatively Cap behaves, the more outrageous you become. If the two of you link lives, there's a risk you'll become caricatures of yourselves. Keep sight of what you do have in common: respect for working toward a goal. Aquarius, stop acting like a teenager and Capricorn will stop behaving like a grandparent.

♓ ♑ *Pisces with Capricorn* Pisceans see things through the comfortable blur of a myopic person who left his contact lenses at home—permanently. Now, what do Capricorns represent? Reality. Cap, if you use phrases like "reality check" too often, you'll check on Pisces only to discover he or she is gone. Pisces can bring the magic of creativity to your world. You, in turn, may provide a foundation that the Fish finds comforting. Even your tendency to work long hours can be a plus. Fish, you need time alone to recharge your batteries. It helps you reconnect with your charming side, a side, by the way, that's much prized by Capricorn (partly because it's much prized by others, too). You two can get along well, especially if Cap makes the effort to be more physically demonstrative. After all, Capricorn, you don't have to do it in public.

11 *the humanitarian heartthrob*

AQUARIUS—THE WATER BEARER,
January 21–February 19

≈ AQUARIUS'S INTERNET DATING PROFILE

Q: Favorite movie
A: *Angels in America*. Technically, it's a play and a miniseries, but I don't believe in slapping labels on things. It should have been a feature film.

THE REAL ANSWER: *Angels in America*

Q: Favorite color
A: Electric blue

THE REAL ANSWER: Electric blue

Q: Favorite book
A: A collection of poetry by Byron

THE REAL ANSWER: *Don Juan*, Byron's masterpiece. But I like anything of his. I heard that if you quote poetry to someone, they'll fall into bed with you.

Q: Favorite classic song
A: "I Can't Give You Anything but Love, Baby"

THE REAL ANSWER: "I Can't Give You Anything but Love, Baby." Well, I can, but I won't. You might get the idea that this relationship is permanent.

Q: Favorite drink
A: Domestic sparkling wine is nice, and I like bottled water, too—but not at the same time, of course.

THE REAL ANSWER: To hell with domestic so-called champagne. Give me Dom Perignon. To show my solidarity with the masses, I'll drink it from a paper cup.

Q: What is your ideal home?
A: An apartment. I'm committed to finding security in temporary arrangements.

THE REAL ANSWER: That depends on whether or not last night's lover let me sleep over.

Q: Where will you be in five years?
A: I don't know. Why do you want to know?

THE REAL ANSWER: Everything changes. Why make plans? I may be bonkers but I'm not that crazy.

Getting to Know Aquarius

Note to reader: If this chapter feels quirky and scattered, it's because it's about Aquarians. It's good to know what your life will be like when you fall for one. Several stereotypes are associated with Aquarians. One is that they're 1960s-type activists who never work because they're too busy agitating with dropouts in sit-ins. Yes, many Water Bearers are humanitarians with an ingrained social conscience. However, more complex than a snappy slogan on a sign, they possess many fascinating facets that are just waiting to be explored by you. Does this mean Aquarius is just a variation of split-personality Gemini? No, Aquarians are a paradox: nonconformists who'll work within the system, fervently detached, and shockingly sexual yet short on passion. And if you become involved with one romantically, what does this mean? It means you're in for the ride of your life.

What's in This Relationship for You

Aquarius has a lot to offer. Read on to see what lies in store.

Relief from routine

Obviously, much excitement and adventure will spice up your daily life. Living with the Water Bearer is never dull. Forward-thinking Aquarius is different from anyone you've ever dated. Expect IMs when you're online and text messages when your cell phone is turned on. You'll be invited to go, sans umbrella, for walks on rainy afternoons. There'll be spur-of-the-moment flights to exotic places.

Sounds great, doesn't it? But remember your lover's ever-present companion: the Aquarius paradox. It will affect everything in your relationship.

Relief from Aquarius's constant presence

Perhaps you relish the Water Bearer's company, and you thought he or she got off on yours, too. But Aquarians can be hard to understand. After the flurry of short-but-sweet messages that your techie lover sent, now you're hearing nothing. You'd come to depend on those surprise trips; then, unexpectedly, your passport has started gathering dust.

What happened? Did Aquarius forget you or become distracted like Gemini? No, Aquarius is dedicating time to other important activities. The Water Bearer is boning up on how to lobby against a state bill that threatens to limit park hours. You'll also find out he is taking weekend road trips in support of a threatened union walkout by airline pilots. But wait, there's more: Aquarius is spending quality alone time with his computer . . . and also with one of his other lovers. Oops! You weren't aware that Aquarius has several on the string? Well, he didn't say you were the only one; you naturally assumed it to be true. Take comfort in the fact that you're not alone. The others don't know about you, either—yet.

 LESSON Aquarius maintains an active outside life that has nothing to do with you. No matter how close you become, portions of that life will always be off-limits.

Where does this quandary leave you? Perhaps exploring the human embodiment of the Aquarian paradox—Lord Byron—will help you understand. We'll travel to Regency England. Imagine that lovely land with its rolling hills, stately homes, and violent squabbles in Parliament. Prince George has taken over as regent now that his father has been declared mad after attempts to cure him failed. Even such modern medical remedies as bleeding and the application of leeches didn't work. Neither does the Prince. He decides to become a leech himself, using state money to buy clothes, mistresses, and silly-looking buildings.

Lord Byron, as you undoubtedly know if you didn't snore your way through lectures on the Romantic poets, was an aristocratic revolutionary who fought for the underdog at a time when titled people treated the lower classes almost as well as four-legged dogs. Byron was a rebel with a sense of duty, a warrior who wrote poetry, and a promiscuous prude. Is it any wonder you have trouble keeping up with what's going on with your own Aquarius? Let's take our experiment a bit further.

Byron, entangled in his most notorious affairs while in Venice, also found time to write a few poems. Let's send him to Venice, California, and see how he fares. Pay close attention: you'll learn valuable lessons about a modern Aquarian's character and whether he's an artiste or an academic.

The Regency rebel awakens from a daze. Perhaps all of the extra wine he drank as he supped the night before is still affecting him—or maybe it's a strike on the head received during battle. For once, Byron is totally confused. He's wearing a flowing white shirt, brown breeches, and a belt that holds his sword. His eye catches a bevy of half-clad young women. With a toss of his shoulder-length hair, he nods. "This is indeed a fine place, with wenches so openly displayed. But where do the ladies of quality reside?" he asks. Perhaps he will encounter Shelly at a literary salon, and they can have a roaring good time talking about rival poets.

Byron spies a large building. "There's an impressive edifice. I shall make enquiries there." As he enters, he sees a lovely young lady. "I wonder why she is imprisoned in a box labeled 'Information?' Where is her needlework? I shall liberate her from this intolerable tyranny."

BYRON "Madam, I have lost my way. Where is the battlefield?"
INFORMATION LADY "Hey, just head for Hollywood. There are wars going on all the time, and I don't mean on the sound stages."
BYRON "Then perhaps you can direct me to a salon."
INFORMATION LADY (AFTER GLANCING AT HIS HAIR) "Sure. You could use a good stylist."

Byron prepares to draw his sword in defense of his literary style, when the lovely lady speaks again.

INFORMATION LADY "Hey, calm down. I like that retro look."
BYRON (A LAND WARRIOR WHO IS NOW TOTALLY AT SEA, THINKING A CUP OF HEADY STIMULANT WOULD DO HIM GOOD) "Can you direct me to a coffee house?"
INFORMATION LADY "You've got to be kidding. Just turn around, and look out that window."

BYRON "I thank you. I fight for the rights of the lower orders, but it would behoove you to learn the correct way to address your betters. You may call me Lord Byron. You may also visit me when you are next in England. Now I shall escort you from this place. Quickly, while the jailers are absent."

INFORMATION LADY "I don't get off for lunch until noon. Thanks anyway."

BYRON "Your servant, madam."

INFORMATION LADY (SHAKING HER HEAD) "Jeez—actors."

You have just witnessed the contradictions inherent in Aquarians. Byron will rescue a lady from imprisonment, yet think less of her for leaving her needlepoint at home. He'll also pull rank as a lord, pointing out to a lady her lack of manners, then take his leave, saying, "Your servant, Madam." Maybe Aquarians aren't from another planet, just another time.

 LESSON When you become more than superficially acquainted with an Aquarius, you'll feel as disoriented as Lord Byron in twenty-first-century Venice, California.

How to Attract Aquarius

Use an original approach
Since Aquarians are unconventional, they'll notice it if you use an imaginative way to connect. Maybe you and Aquarius work for the

same company but in different departments. At an interdepartmental mixer, approach your romantic prey. "Hi. I've seen you around the building. I could flirt with you or use flattery, but I'm sure you've heard it all before. I'd like to get to know you. Here's my mobile number." Aquarius replies, "Why don't we leave and do something fun?"

 LESSON Cut through conventional courtship rituals, and Aquarius will be interested.

Suggest an unconventional date

Maybe you've spotted an Aquarius you're familiar with at a poetry reading. You know each other well enough to go out for coffee or dinner, but the relationship hasn't progressed further yet. After you've gotten your books signed, suggest going out for a coffee. This sounds like the opening to a run-of-the-mill date, but you're planning to add a twist.

YOU "Let's take my car."
AQUARIUS (AS YOU PASS THE NEAREST COFFEE BAR) "You missed your turn."
YOU (SMILING MYSTERIOUSLY) "No, I didn't."

Pick up a couple of coffees at a convenience store, then head for the airport. The mere sound of planes is a reminder that there are other places to visit, and that you're game for any of them.

 LESSON Adventurousness turns Aquarius on. Now you're in—welcome to Aquarius's world.

The Aquarius Deal Breaker: Self-centeredness

Aquarius is a detached air sign. Unlike the water signs, the Water Bearer runs from introspection faster than a Cancerian darts to a donut sale. It doesn't mean Aquarius won't examine his or her flaws or problems. He just doesn't want to wallow in them, and won't like it if you do.

The Committed Relationship: You Got What You Wanted; Here's How to Keep It

Be your rational rebel's main cause

Aquarius is rational, a helpful quality when sorting out problems, although not so desirable when you crave a searing emotional and physical connection. However, there's a prime opportunity here to use Aquarius's knowledge and proclivities to your advantage. Remember our rebel? Your Aquarius may bear no resemblance to Byron; he may sport a buzz cut and tacky taste in poetry. But he's almost as impulsive as an Aries. Rebellious to boot, he knows more about technological gadgets than any nonprofessional you know.

Be impulsive

Let's say your goal is to add heat to your sexual encounters. Don't divulge your plan; Aquarius likes impulsiveness. Go to a shop that sells sex toys, and choose something that requires assembly. Then, while he is adding another memory card to his computer, spread out your little project on the floor next to him. He'll notice that although you've read the instructions twice, you haven't gotten very far in assembling your toy. Aquarius interjects, "What do you have there? Maybe I can help you put it together."

You just sit back and let Aquarius do his job. Suddenly he gets an idea, "Let's try it out now." At last, you can have your wicked way. Be sure to remind Aquarius that his Boy Scout merit badges in rope tying need never go to waste.

Do's and Don'ts in the Aquarius Mating Game
With someone born under such a tolerant sign, you'd think there would be no "nos." You'd be mistaken.

Don't call a cell phone a cell phone. It sounds restrictive—as in prison cell. Your Aquarius might think it represents a desire on your part to cage him or her. Call it a mobile phone instead.

Don't issue ultimatums. You are asking for a swift end to your relationship if you tell Aquarius he or she must choose between you and someone or something else. On principle, Aquarius will choose the other, no matter how much he or she loves you. In his mind, if you're going to ask him to stop seeing other people occasionally, what's your next demand? You might even go so far as to ask him to give up DSL or TiVo.

Don't tell Aquarius what to do. Try making suggestions instead. Let's say Aquarius isn't the most efficient car-maintenance person. She may have earned an engineering degree, but she can't remember that it's time for an oil change and that unless the radiator is filled with antifreeze the upcoming blizzard might leave her without wheels. Instead of taking charge and making an appointment at the car dealership, take her shopping with you. Instead, say, "I have to tinker with my car before the storm hits. Want to come to the store with me?" Aquarius is restless and agrees. Then, she'll realize she should prepare her own car.

Do retain your independence. Like Sadge, Aquarius dislikes clingy people.

Do cultivate interests outside the relationship. Otherwise, the Water Bearer's notorious independence will leave you sitting home alone on many a Friday night—even if you do make it to the committed-relationship stage.

You Want Out: Ways to Leave Your Loser

Aquarius was fun, but you couldn't stand all that humanitarianism and sharing. Unfortunately for monogamy, your partner's ideology about freedom extended to relationships. You were aware of that particular quirk at the beginning, and thought you could handle it, but eventually it went too far. You had hoped that being such a humanitarian, he wouldn't sleep with your friends. As you confront Aquarius about this, you find him twisting the sheets with someone else.

YOU "What the hell is this?"

AQUARIUS "Oh, hi. I'm gathering data for my protest against artificially–induced suntans. What's wrong with you?"

YOU "Nothing. There's something wrong with you, though. You no longer have a place to live."

Perhaps you're in the mood to add some cheap shots to the end of this relationship with a bang. Check out the following for some choice words.

- "You're about as revolutionary as my fundamentalist grandmother."
- "Guess what? I didn't vote in the last election."
- "You love having groups of people around you. You call them friends. Well, I don't believe in friends."
- "I lied. I have more friends than you do, and I've slept with most of mine and all of yours, too."
- Finish off with something that would send Lord Byron into a fatal swoon: "I'm about to marry a Taurus and start voting Republican."

Bliss or Bloodshed? How Your Sign Fits with Aquarius

♈ ♒ **Aries with Aquarius** See Chapter 1, Aquarius with Aries.

♉ ♒ **Taurus with Aquarius** See Chapter 2, Aquarius with Taurus.

♊ ♒ **Gemini with Aquarius** See Chapter 3, Aquarius with Gemini.

♋ ♒ **Cancer with Aquarius** See Chapter 4, Aquarius with Cancer.

♌ ♒ **Leo with Aquarius** See Chapter 5, Aquarius with Leo.

♍ ♒ **Virgo with Aquarius** See Chapter 6, Aquarius with Virgo.

♎ ♒ **Libra with Aquarius** See Chapter 7, Aquarius with Libra.

♏ ♒ **Scorpio with Aquarius** See Chapter 8, Aquarius with Scorpio.

♐ ♒ **Sagittarius with Aquarius** See Chapter 9, Aquarius with Sagittarius.

♑ ♒ **Capricorn with Aquarius** See Chapter 10, Aquarius with Capricorn.

♒ ♒ **Aquarius with Aquarius** Here are two whirlwinds in one relationship. Readers, place your bets. Even cautious Capricorn is calculating the odds, and conservative Taurus is laying out cash as if Seabiscuit has come back to life and is racing at the Santa Anita Race Track. Aquariuses, what will you do? Perpetuate the stereotype by starting a commune? Or will you channel your mental energy into other areas like social welfare and how to build a time machine so that you can see what the Supreme Court will look like in thirty years? You've got the ability and inclination to embrace either project—maybe both. After all, since when were sex and politics mutually exclusive?

♓ ♒ **Pisces with Aquarius** Private Pisces enjoys the alone time that's always available in a relationship with an Aquarius. You don't mind the Water Bearer's tendency toward debauchery. Actually, you've got a few tricks of your own that your lover has never seen. It's nice to be given a lot of room. Aquarius, you appreciate the similarities between yourself and Pisces, especially when those related to freedom of movement. What you don't like is the Fish's sneaky ways. You're open about your other relationships. Why isn't Pisces? Because it's fun to keep secrets. Cut your mate some slack. Pisces is intensely emotional, and your trying to manage emotional issues in a logical way doesn't always work. Let Pisces coax you into exploring your emotional side. Yes, you do have one. As an adventurous Aquarius, what's holding you back? Are you afraid of losing control? Dare to explore your own mind. Lord Byron did.

12 *the shape-shifting soul mate*

PISCES—THE FISHES, February 20–March 19

♓ PISCES'S INTERNET DATING PROFILE

Q: Favorite movie
A: *Captains Courageous*

THE REAL ANSWER: *Lifeboat*. Hitchcock knows about mystery, the sea, and getting lost.

Q: Favorite color
A: Blue. It's the usual answer. Besides, it looks good on blondes, brunettes, and redheads.

THE REAL ANSWER: Aqua, the color of the Caribbean

Q: Favorite classic song
A: "In the Mood"

THE REAL ANSWER: "Heartbreaker." The Stones know the score about romance and tell it like it is. It's a good thing, too, because I won't.

Q: Favorite book

A: *The Brothers Karamazov*

THE REAL ANSWER: *The Brothers Karamazov*. Dostoyevsky is tremendously tragic. What a turn-on. The Grand Inquisitor scene poses deep existential questions, and it gives me the willies like all my exes did when they gave me the third degree. Good reminder of when to bail.

Q: What is your ideal home?

A: Any place I can hang my hat; preferably by a lake or the sea

THE REAL ANSWER: A real apartment. I'll keep a P.O. box, too, and an unlisted number. I'll also have a hideout where I can be alone when I want. When I don't . . . well, there's room for company.

P.S. Pisces's posted photo will be visually enhanced—just the background, though. Real life is so inartistic.

Getting to Know Pisces

Getting to know Pisces is a fine art. As an artist in the gallery of love, you'll have no problem reconciling two images of the Fishes (Pisces does, however). One depiction relates to the sea, with all its depth, mystery, and danger; the other is connected to the world of art and illusion. Let's begin the artistic journey. Your soul mate awaits.

You may be familiar with the myth of the Sirens. These maidens used their beautiful voices to lure hapless, intrepid sailors to them. Spellbound, the sailors steered their vessels in the direction of the melodies only to be shipwrecked on rocks. Warning: You could experience a similar crash, but not before Pisces shows you a good time.

Let's make an entrance into the art world, a place filled with beauty that stimulates many senses. Chopin nocturnes play softly in the background as you enter this Piscean palace of illusion. In one room is your gateway to the world of film. Silent or mid-twentieth-century classics are on view. You can also be dazzled by up-to-the-second movies that star special effects instead of actual actors. Entranced, you enter another space that is filled with sculpture, photographs, and paintings. The latter hold special interest for you. Could that be Monet's *Water Lilies*? You're looking at a genuine Impressionist painting. It's dreamily painted, beautifully yet blurrily colored, and extremely expensive—kind of like life with Pisces.

In the middle of the room is compassionate, empathetic, mysterious Pisces. Drawn in already, you wonder if the vision standing before you is real or phantom, a gentle fish or closet shark? Connect; it's the only way to find out if you'll win the lover's lottery or end up in divorce court.

What's in This Relationship for You

You've met your soul mate. Just as one blood type is considered a universal donor, there's an astrological sign that's the universal soul mate. How can this be true of Pisces? First, the Fish actually has a soul. Second, Pisces can be all things to all people. A Fish on the lookout for a new lover is irresistible. At first, Pisces can be everything you ever dreamed of.

 LESSON If everything seems perfect, it probably isn't.

Yes, there can be problems. You never know whether you'll be aboard the good ship Lollipop or the Titanic. But once you've melded with the Fish, the benefits of the relationship will be legion. Who else listens so patiently to your problems? Who else so gladly gets up in the middle of the night to buy cold medicine and deliver it to you with loving care? Who else is so easily conned into running this errand just so you can seduce the Fish upon his or her return?

 LESSON Pisces's good qualities leave her wide open to manipulation—or so it seems.

Refrain from becoming too smug. Pisceans possess numerous defense mechanisms to protect them from scurvy tricks. Before you pack your bags for a power trip, thinking triumphantly about the seemingly free ticket in your hand, stop to consider. Not only will you swim with a part-time shark, but you can turn into one, too. Pisces is clearly a catch, but when you're playing the manipulation game, there's a hidden catch. Pisces likes to do things for you; it satisfies his need to be useful. It also presents the opportunity for him or her to seduce you, which was his plan all along. Still feel clever?

How to Attract Pisces

Pisces is so susceptible, he or she is easy to seduce—physically, that is. But one must first meet and talk to the Fishes before physical seduction takes place. Pisces can sense a truly compatible mate from 20,000 leagues under the sea. Since Pisces is especially drawn to certain personality traits, it's important to know what they are—and to remember that Pisces will recognize the presence or absence of those traits in you.

Luckily for you, though, she will don blinders if you attract her in alternative ways. Read on to see how you can nudge Pisces into blocking her own perception. Then you can continue dating, and either become what the Fish wants or persuade the Fish to do what you want.

Act emotionally open

The Fish enjoys a love challenge, but his sensitivity requires someone who's willing to be open. If he intuits a barbed wire fence topped with razor blades surrounding your heart, he'll be reluctant to open his. (This is okay if you're just interested in a romp.) Make a mental note that the Fish is ambiguous and revels in complications. Indicate your emotional door is open, but only far enough for him to slip in. Try doing the following if you want to spur Pisces into following you.

> **PISCES (TO YOU, OVER COFFEE)** "I like to go ice skating. What do you like to do?"
>
> **YOU** "Ice skating is fun. It makes me sad sometimes, though, because the cold reminds me of what it's like for people who are closed down."
>
> **PISCES (WARMING TO YOUR TAKE ON COLDNESS)** "Yeah, I see what you mean. After we finish here, how about having some dinner?"
>
> **YOU** "That would be lovely, but I have a busy day tomorrow." Just as Pisces thinks you're giving him the brush-off, tell him, "But I'd love to go another time."

 LESSON Indicate you're receptive but don't be a pushover. Pisces likes to skate on thin ice.

Pretend to let your guard down occasionally

Pisces has a passive side, and uses it at his convenience. But he likes to be aggressive about messing with your head. He even relishes messing with his own head. His sharklike tendencies will pop up without notice or invitation. The Fishes tend to know what you want even if you don't. Some would claim it's a result of being psychic or perceptive. Astrology would maintain it stems from the cosmically bestowed gift of relationship paranoia Pisces has practiced happily and masochistically for years. So, where do these aggressive tendencies come from? From the Dorian Gray side of Pisces.

LESSON Pisces isn't always passive. Sometimes the Fish is outrageously aggressive. Learn to cope with both traits, and allow Pisces to screw with your head a few times. Then you can console yourself with thoughts of all the fun you'll have messing with his.

Be enigmatic

Because Pisces is a mystery, he loves to encounter one. There's nothing more intriguing than an enigma. But let's take one neurosis at a time. Prove you're as hard to pin down or uncover as a secret agent. Suppose it's dinner-date night. Should you let Pisces pick you up at your place? No, meet him at the restaurant. Then, after a post-dinner quick kiss, decline to disclose where you live.

PISCES "Maybe you had too much wine. Can I drive you home?"

YOU "I'm fine. Thanks, though."

PISCES "Then I'll just follow you there to make sure you get home safely."

YOU (TO YOURSELF, "NICE TRY.") "No, thanks."

Then just let the unanswered question marinate like a fillet of salmon in teriyaki sauce. Pisces is well acquainted with this maneuver. After gazing at store windows for a few moments, he abandons the fake window-shopping and says good night. You've just created a mystery about your address and indicated you may have other plans after dinner.

LESSON Act enigmatic and you'll stymie Pisces's attempt to penetrate your persona.

Pretend you enjoy long-distance relationships

Now you're "in," and you both want to explore the newly opened possibilities. In love relationships, Pisceans of either gender need to be emotionally connected but feel free to roam around at the same time. Yes, this is another tiresome paradox. The astrological symbol of the sign represents two fish swimming in opposite directions. So what do you expect, consistency? Convince the Fish that you enjoy having lots of space, and you'll appeal to him or her—it means you won't try to keep her on a short leash. As accommodating as any Fish can be, she'll flee at the mere word "leash." Long-distance relationships work great with this sign. The farther away you are geographically, the closer Pisces will stay to you emotionally. Naturally, you'll wonder what other seas the Fish may be exploring. But even if you were cohabiting, you might still wonder about that.

 LESSON Once you've hooked Pisces, leave her dangling on the end of a very long line. It's virtually invisible, unlike a leash.

The Pisces Deal Breaker: Possessiveness

Yes, we've pondered this dilemma. We know the Fishes don't have a wandering eye—they have four wandering eyes. The only suggestions astrology can offer is to allow Pisces room, avoid giving her the third degree, and define your own limits. You already own a door-mat; you don't have to be one.

The Committed Relationship: You Got What You Wanted; Here's How to Keep It

By now, you and Pisces have fulfilled your karmic destiny and hooked up together. You've progressed beyond exchanging kisses to exchanging house keys. Have you made the right decision by meld-ing with a sensitive yet sharklike sign? Astrologers can answer the question only with a word Pisces uses all the time: "Maybe."

Do's and Don'ts in the Pisces Mating Game

Pisces has many great qualities. To keep your relationship fresh, try the following:

Do ask questions politely. And say thank you when Pisces has tapped into her Mary-the-Martyr side and sacrificed something for you.

Do refer to Pisces's creative versions of the truth. As something other than lies, that is.

Do remember to nurture Pisces.

Do give Pisces space. If you don't, the Fish will take it anyway.

Don't be confrontational. Confrontation will piss off a Pisces and make him dematerialize. Just think how that would affect your relationship, not to mention your sex life. It's hard to have actual sex with someone who isn't there. At the same time, don't be a pushover when Pisces has committed a goodly (or ungodly) number of infractions.

Don't underestimate Piscean practicality. Pisces has a reputation for being fuzzy-minded and off in outer space. Just because she's spiritual and can be pulled in two directions doesn't mean there isn't a strong practical streak in her personality. The Fish approaches the practical in a mystical way. She mixes the sacred with the mundane. For example, you'll find her asking for divine intervention in keeping gas bills down and burning incense to cleanse the atmosphere before tackling dirty dishes.

 LESSON If you make fun of Pisces's spiritual-yet-practical ways, he will forgo practicality completely. Then, rather than going with the flow, your Fish will just drift aimlessly. Let him integrate his need for woo-woo into everyday life.

The Committed Relationship: You Got What You Wanted; Here's How to Keep It

It happens to us all. The initial romantic heat cools over time, and you yearn to recapture it. What's the best way to accomplish this?

Play up the anticipation

Put romance on the back burner and be creative about sex. Some signs, like Aries or Aquarius, like for you to spring seduction on them. For example, an Aries would be delighted if, while out on a nighttime walk, you hauled her off into the shrubbery for a quick one. An Aquarius would think it's out of this world to peek into the windows of a swinger's club you'd just driven past (not that swinger's clubs have windows). The point is that your Pisces likes anticipation. Try the following to tantalize the Fish into being hot for you again—not that there's anything in this for you, right?

Pisces is taking you to an elegant dinner party. You've just rung the doorbell.

YOU (AS YOU HEAR THE TAP OF YOUR HOST'S FOOTSTEPS APPROACHING THE DOOR) "Do you remember the black thong underwear you like?"
PISCES "Mmm, yes. My favorite."
YOU "Well, I'm not wearing them."
PISCES (TURNED OFF BY THE IDEA OF YOU SPORTING WHITE GRANNY PANTIES AND SEEMING DISAPPOINTED) "Oh."
YOU "I'm not wearing underwear at all."

Suddenly the door opens, and the host greets you with smiles. Now you can enjoy watching Pisces squirm impatiently through each course. After finishing the crème brûlée, everyone expects your Fish to stay for the usual snifter of postprandial cognac. Instead, Pisces steers you through the house, grabs your coat, and stops only to thank the hosts for a lovely meal.

LESSON Be a tease with Pisces, and you'll be the next lovely meal.

Take risks

These types of risk don't entail gambling with physical safety, but rather with the possibility of being discovered. Pisces gets a charge out of imagining you might be caught with your pants down, literally. Dare the chance.

Again, use anticipation. Tell Pisces in advance about the evening you've planned.

> **YOU** "We'll have a great time. After the movie, we can go up to the couches in the balcony. They're usually roped off on weeknights and maybe nobody will catch us. If that's too public, we'll sneak out into the alleyway and up the outside stairs."
>
> **PISCES** "Yes. And we can use the railing as support—."
>
> **YOU** "Who needs support?"
>
> **PISCES** "Maybe we can go to the gym."

You're wondering how far to go with imagining your stealthy deeds. Pisces is now trying to persuade you to find a dark corner inside a nightclub. You're thinking to yourself, "You've got to be kidding. That's not fun—it's the prelude to an arrest for public lewdness." Keep talking. If you do it well enough, the outrageous schemes might just be short-circuited and you'll find yourself at home saying, "What about the gym?" Pisces answers, "Who needs a gym when you've got a king-sized bed?"

You Want Out: Ways to Leave Your Loser

It didn't work out after all. Pisces grew weary of having to top your manipulative methods and bored with receiving phone calls all the time. Pisces interpreted your efforts to maintain closeness as keeping tabs and hasn't been present, either physically or mentally. The Fish was such a help, so understanding, in the beginning. Then why is it you're the one who is doing all the rescuing? The helper has become the helpless. The Fishes were never much for conversation, but now talk has dwindled down to, "What's for dinner?" and, "When are you going to prune the bushes?"

Other problems have cropped up as well and even the most creative solutions no longer work. Also, Pisces misbehaved. While the Fish is out doing the laundry, you find out she's doing it with her ex. And it's the ex's fault the laundry is dirty in the first place. You decide the Pisces astrological symbol is two fish *sneaking* off in different directions and realize you have limits.

It's over. The feelings are gone, leaving mere indifference, thank God. Not all news is good, though. This is the most complicated ditching you'll ever have to do. You can't just toss off a few insults, as you would to Leo. With sharpened intuition, Pisces will sense you don't want him around. That's when he'll badger you with the tenacity of Taurus and the force of Aries. This is such un-Piscean behavior, you'll wonder if he lied about his birth date. After all, he fibbed about everything else. Pisces loves you. Simply cannot do without you. The romance is back with a vengeance, the promise of great sex is more fervent than ever, and he's started a twelve-step course to help him beat the fidelity-fibbery habit.

What can you do? What should you do? *What are you going to do?* Calm down. Eventually her roving eyes will pull the Fish in another direction. In the meantime, how do you cope? It would take the creativity of another super-Pisces to come up with fifteen ways to leave this loser. And why bother? Don't even think about it.

Bliss or Bloodshed? How Your Sign Fits with Pisces

♈ ♓ *Aries with Pisces* See Chapter 1, Pisces with Aries.

♉ ♓ *Taurus with Pisces* See Chapter 2, Pisces with Taurus.

♊ ♓ *Gemini with Pisces* See Chapter 3, Pisces with Gemini.

♋ ♓ *Cancer with Pisces* See Chapter 4, Pisces with Cancer.

♌ ♓ *Leo with Pisces* See Chapter 5, Pisces with Leo.

♍ ♓ *Virgo with Pisces* See Chapter 6, Pisces with Virgo.

♎ ♓ *Libra with Pisces* See Chapter 7, Pisces with Libra.

♏ ♓ *Scorpio with Pisces* See Chapter 8, Pisces with Scorpio.

♐ ♓ *Sagittarius with Pisces* See Chapter 9, Pisces with Sagittarius.

♑ ♓ **Capricorn with Pisces** See Chapter 10, Pisces with Capricorn.

♒ ♓ **Aquarius with Pisces** See Chapter 11, Pisces with Aquarius.

♓ ♓ **Pisces with Pisces** This match could go either way, depending on the personalities of the Pisceans involved. You're both alike in that you can read each other; you're both interested in architecture or painting or learning more about anything in this life. This isn't your first life together; there was definitely a connection in a previous life.

Your main challenge is complacency—the relationship could get too comfortable. Otherwise, it's mutually supportive in that you can take turns being the leader. You have the chance to be a Fish or shark and remain guilt free. Just find a Virgo to help you coordinate your alternating stints as the shark.

conclusion

The zodiac is no longer a twisting mystery; it's a veritable Love Boat! Remember when you were put off by Aries's headstrong ways, not to mention those very, very sharp horns? No more; now you know that putting up a little resistance to the Ram can stun her into submission. Oh, and there was a time when you were afraid you couldn't tempt truculent Taurus from his sofa; these days, you know that dangling a treat—edible, sexual, or both—in front of the Bull's eyes goes a long way.

What about the devilish duo, Gemini? Once, Gem's flighty, dualistic nature had you in a muddle; but you've learned how to beat Gem at his own game: variety. Perhaps you moved on to a cautious Cancer, and wondered how to keep her claws at bay; today, you know that with the Crab, a lot of reassurance goes a long way.

Then there's that life of the party, Leo, who you were sure would never notice you. Now you've lured him in with lavish compliments—and your own sassy style. And how could you forget Virgo, so well versed in the art of home—and mate—improvement? You learned to pique her interest by pretending you could use a little work yourself—in the bedroom, that is.

Let's not ignore the oh-so-fair-and-balanced Libra, whom you reeled in like an expert by showing off your intelligence, your romantic side, and, most of all, your tact. Moody, brooding, super-sexed Scorpio: now there was a challenge. But you learned to dodge his jealousy bullets like a pro, and the results were well worth it. At first you thought you'd never trap a globe-trotting Sadge, but you snapped up a lovely Archer after all; showing her your spontaneous side did the trick.

Perhaps you'd been coveting a conservative Capricorn. You're an old pro now; after wowing him with your impeccable taste and elegant manners, you persuaded the Goat to focus his intense energy on you—and reaped the bedtime benefits. And when you were lusting after Aquarius, you puzzled over how to keep her in one place long enough to flirt with her, but after you convinced her that you're the most creative, unconventional fellow going, she made you her favorite cause. Pisces is such a slippery Fish, you thought you'd never hook him—but after you disguised yourself as a mystery, he was certain that you were as ocean-deep as he, and came swimming right into your waiting fins.

You've learned to finesse each sign to get just what you need from him or her—and from your relationship. Now that you've got your master's degree in the art of manipulation, you're ready to take on the entire zodiac. Congratulations!